# CIGAR BOX
# GUITARS

# CIGAR BOX
# GUITARS

## The Ultimate DIY Guide for Makers and Players of the Handmade Music Revolution

### David Sutton

Fox Chapel
PUBLISHING

*Special thanks to everyone who supported me and helped me along the way; most importantly, to my wife, Tia, and daughter, Alisha, who did without me a fair bit when I was away and when I was on deadline.*

*Thanks to Peg Couch and all the good people at Fox Chapel Publishing. Important thanks also go to Max Shores, who gave me substantial entree into the cigar box guitar community, and whose documentary film,* Songs Inside the Box, *was as good an introduction to this world as I can imagine. Thanks especially to Bill Jehle and Shane Speal, both of whom went far beyond the call in helping me wade through vast collections of cigar box guitars for the gallery sections; thanks to Ted Crocker for his generosity with clearing up technical mysteries; and to B.G. "Yogi" Yovovich for his editorial contributions and guidance along the way. Thanks, too, to Scott Grandstaff of Happy Camp, California, for being my favorite old tool resource for nearly two decades.*

---

*Cigar Box Guitars* is an original work, first published in 2012 by Fox Chapel Publishing Company, Inc., East Petersburg, PA. The patterns contained herein are copyrighted by the author. Readers may make copies of these patterns for personal use. The patterns themselves, however, are not to be duplicated for resale or distribution under any circumstances. Any such copying is a violation of copyright law.

ISBN 978-1-56523-547-2

Library of Congress Cataloging-in-Publication Data

Sutton, David, 1958-
Cigar box guitars / David Sutton. -- 1st ed.
     p. cm.
Includes index.
ISBN 978-1-56523-547-2
1. Cigar box guitar--Construction. 2. Cigar box guitar makers--Interviews. I. Title.
ML1015.G9S88 2012
787.87'192--dc23
                    2011041194

To learn more about the other great books from Fox Chapel Publishing, or to find a retailer near you, call toll-free 800-457-9112 or visit us at *www.FoxChapelPublishing.com*.

**Note to Authors:** We are always looking for talented authors to write new books. Please send a brief letter describing your idea to Acquisition Editor, 1970 Broad Street, East Petersburg, PA 17520.

Printed in China
First printing

Because working with wood and other materials inherently includes the risk of injury and damage, this book cannot guarantee that creating the projects in this book is safe for everyone. For this reason, this book is sold without warranties or guarantees of any kind, expressed or implied, and the publisher and the author disclaim any liability for any injuries, losses, or damages caused in any way by the content of this book or the reader's use of the tools needed to complete the projects presented here. The publisher and the author urge all readers to thoroughly review each project and to understand the use of all tools before beginning any project.

"In a world filled with high-tech, soulless devices, we build low-tech and soulful instruments. We breathe life into junk and give it a voice to sing to others' hearts. For me, there is no greater thrill than that first strum of a CBG [cigar box guitar] that was built by my own hand."

**-SHAWN, CIGAR BOX NATION**

# CONTENTS

# ABOUT THE AUTHOR

When he's not building cigar box guitars, David Sutton specializes in photographing dogs and families with their pets at his studio in Evanston, Illinois.

Coming from a long line of teachers and tradesmen, perhaps it was inevitable that David Sutton would write a book showing people how to build something.

During his quarter century as a professional photographer, David has always managed to steal time for handiwork, one way or another. Whether restoring old hand tools, carving wood, making jewelry, or building little guitars, he has always found something there that couldn't be replaced by his more practical pursuits.

David gets a similar satisfaction from his charitable efforts (primarily through Sutton Studios), which have helped to raise over a million dollars for dozens of animal and human welfare organizations.

And now this: a book that he crafted for many months and still can hardly believe is here. He sincerely hopes that you enjoy reading and using this book even half as much as he enjoyed putting it together.

www.cigarboxguitarbook.com • www.suttonstudios.com • www.davidbsutton.com

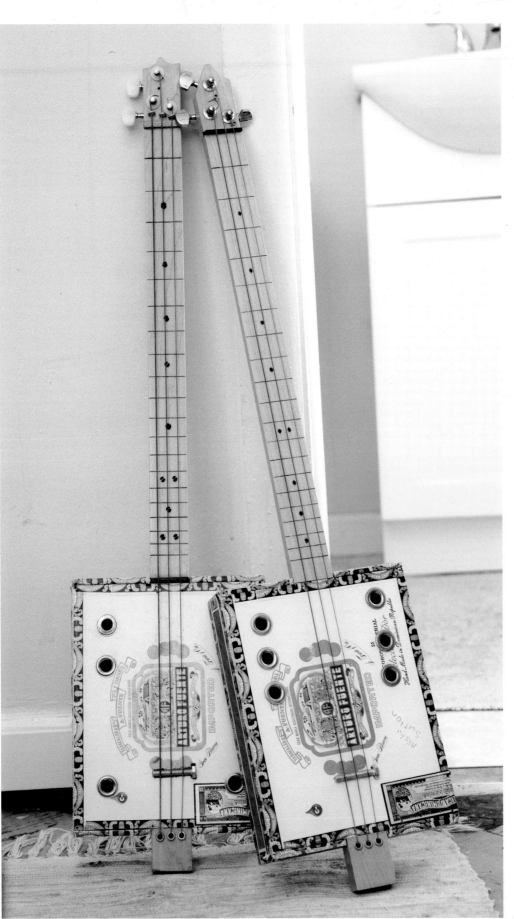

**My first cigar box guitars.**
I built these two guitars side by side (one for me and one for my daughter) using salvaged tuners and some maple off-cuts from a neighbor's remodeling project. Both guitars are acoustic. The good news about these two cigar box guitars is that they sound great, owing in part to the fortuitous choice of maple for the necks. I made my headstocks a bit too short; lesson learned.

**Numero Uno, nut side detail.** OK, the slot was a little sloppy...

**Numero Uno, nut.** I used a piece of natural horn for this nut. The piece was too wide, but too small to cut down, so I created a slot for it to drop into. The brass screw acts as a string tree.

"I like to build dem cigar box geetars. Gives me sumpin' to do when I'm too drunk to fish—yup."

—BONE DADDY,
HANDMADE MUSIC CLUBHOUSE

**Numero Uno, detail.** I used brass tarp grommets to trim out my sound holes, and brass eyelets from Tandy Leather to line the string anchor holes. I cut into the box lid to sink the bolt's head so that it would lie flat.

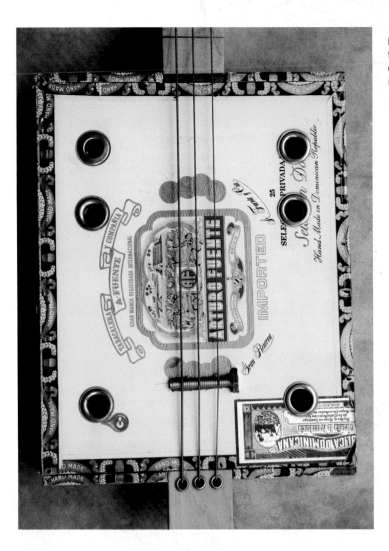

**Number Two, detail.** I used the same strategies with this one as with Numero Uno; I just reconfigured the soundholes.

**Number Two, headstock.** I made this nut out of a piece of oak dowel. This time I used eye screws for my string trees.

**Number Two, bridge.** I sunk the head of this bolt as well, so the bridge would be flat.

**Sisters build.** Splitting
a set of six (3 left/3 right)
tuners between two three-string
guitars gave me the idea to
make this pair—one fretted,
one fretless—out of matching
boxes. I cut the headstocks
so they mirror one another.

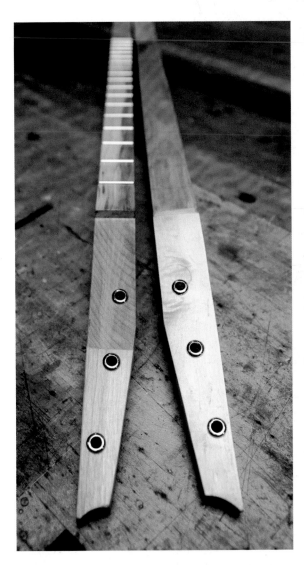

**Sisters, neck.** I used some ancient maple for the necks. This maple had done service as a shelf in a very fancy house for at least a hundred years before being discarded during a remodeling project. I used scarf joints to angle the headstocks. You can see the joint in the neck on the left. The headstock for the fretless guitar was just thin enough to make me nervous, so I overlaid a ¼" (6mm) piece of curly maple for added strength. The fretted guitar has a cherry fretboard.

**Sisters, mirrored headstocks.** Headstocks of finished guitars.

**Sisters, tail piece.** I mounted a piece of rosewood to the end of each box to give the string anchors a solid base. I used brass hinges for the string anchors.

**Sisters, sound hole.** These La Aroma de Cuba cigar boxes come with a presentation overleaf inside. I moved each overleaf so it would be visible through the sound hole.

**Sisters, just before final assembly.** Each has a piezo pickup under the bridge and a volume control knob. Some builders argue that the volume control isn't necessary with a piezo because the output is quite low. Piezos are notorious for feeding back, though, and I like to have a volume control to dial it down whenever I get feedback.

**Fretless Sister, nut/headstock overlay.** Here, you can see the bolt and the curly maple overlay.

**Sisters, nut detail.** I used a bolt as the nut for the fretless guitar. The fret lines were cut in with a marking knife and darkened up when I finished the neck with an oil finish.

**Fretted Sister, nut and fretboard.** This angle shows the fretboard and nut positioning clearly.

**Sisters, nut detail two.** I used a piece of horn for the nut of the fretted guitar. The fretboard is ¼" (6mm) cherry.

"Each cigar box is different and presents different challenges to the builder. The sheer number of possible components makes it easy to make each guitar completely different... 'What can I use for a bridge? How about this door hinge for a tailpiece?' A trip down the aisle at the home improvement store turns into a CBG parts locating expedition."

—*IGGY, CIGAR BOX NATION*

# Foreword:
# WHY I BUILD CIGAR BOX GUITARS

## BY MARK FRAUENFELDER

I get bored easily. I typically develop an interest in something (drumming, sewing, model rocketry, kite building, coffee roasting, etc.), pursue it gung-ho for 18 months, then trail off. It doesn't bother me that I go through these cycles of interest and boredom, because I enjoy learning about new things. When I started building cigar box guitars in 2008, I assumed I'd want nothing to do with them by 2010. But nearly four years and a dozen cigar box guitars, ukuleles, and diddley bows later, I'm as excited as I ever was.

I'm not sure why my enthusiasm for cigar box instruments hasn't flagged, like it has with every other hobby I've picked up. But I have a hunch it's because cigar box guitar making possesses the following qualities:

★ ★ ★ ★ ★ ★ **1** ★ ★ ★ ★ ★ ★

### EVERY CIGAR BOX GUITAR HAS A PERSONALITY

Unlike the guitars you'll find at retail stores that sell cookie-cutter instruments, no two cigar box guitars sound the same. I have no idea what the guitar I'm currently building is going to sound like until I string it up and start playing it.

The surprise of hearing its sound for the first time (and tweaking the instrument to improve the sound) is a treat that hasn't gotten old, and I suspect won't get old.

---

**THE SURPRISE OF HEARING A CBG'S SOUND FOR THE FIRST TIME (AND TWEAKING THE INSTRUMENT TO IMPROVE THE SOUND) IS A TREAT THAT HASN'T GOTTEN OLD, AND I SUSPECT WON'T GET OLD.**

---

★ ★ ★ ★ ★ ★ **2** ★ ★ ★ ★ ★ ★

## CIGAR BOX GUITARS CAN BE MADE FROM ALL KINDS OF JUNK

Another great thing about cigar box guitars, which you will discover when you read David's book, is that they can be built using junk drawer components. Building CBGs will improve your resourcefulness, ingenuity, and creativity. Some of my most pleasurable builds have happened when I found that I was missing a particular component, and was forced to come up with a makeshift solution. For example, when I once discovered that I was missing a piece of plastic I had hoped to use for a bridge, I resorted to using a pencil stub instead. Now, pencil stubs are a standard component on my instruments. If you start building CBGs, you will begin to look at the world as a giant spare-parts bin.

★ ★ ★ ★ ★ ★ **3** ★ ★ ★ ★ ★ ★

## MISTAKES OFTEN IMPROVE CIGAR BOX GUITARS

Once I made a measurement error while marking the fret locations on a CBG, and I ended up sawing a fret slot in the wrong place. I was about to throw the neck away, but then I decided to try filling in the bad slot with putty made from a mixture of sawdust and wood glue. The putty worked, but it looked ugly. Again, I was tempted to toss the whole thing and start over. As a last ditch effort to cover up the scar, I painted the fretboard a bright shade of green. I liked the paint job, and now I often paint my CBG fretboards a bright color. I probably wouldn't have ever started doing that had I not made that measurement error. Cigar box guitars are also quite forgiving in the way you build them. I've made them with crooked frets, cracked necks, upside-down tuning pegs, and worse. But when I string them up and play them, lo and behold, they sound OK!

★ ★ ★ ★ ★ ★ **4** ★ ★ ★ ★ ★ ★

## YOU TRULY OWN YOUR CIGAR BOX GUITAR.

The best thing about making cigar box guitars is the satisfaction I receive from using my hands to make something that I understand. I really own it. If it breaks I know how to fix it. If I want to modify it, I'm not nervous about stripping it down and adding or removing components. If I screw up totally and ruin it, so what? Now I have the opportunity to build another!

David's book is a wonderful introduction to the world of cigar box guitars and cigar box guitar makers. After browsing through the hundreds of photos of guitars built by David and other luminaries of the cigar box guitar world, my head is spinning with ideas that I plan to swipe and incorporate into my own future builds. I'm thrilled David has written this book, because it's going to introduce so many people to this most fascinating musical instrument. Happy building, and happy strumming!

**BIO:** Mark Frauenfelder is the editor-in-chief of *Make* magazine and the founder of the popular Boing Boing blog. He was an editor at *Wired* from 1993–1998, and is the author of six books, including *Made By Hand: Searching for Meaning in a Throwaway World*. See *http://bit.ly/madebyhands*.

# PREFACE

In 2006, when she was about five, my daughter started taking an interest in my guitars. I thought it would be nice if she had a guitar of her own that she could use without her dad "hovering." I recalled my own dad mentioning cigar box guitars to me when I was a kid, so I started poking around the Internet to see if I could find some ideas.

My search engines turned up perhaps two modest references to cigar box guitars (CBGs). I had imagined something made from a cardboard box and using rubber bands for strings. Instead, I found instructions for building primitive instruments capable of making real music.

I built my daughter and myself a pair of three-string guitars using wooden cigar boxes, salvaged pieces of 1x2 maple from a rehab project next door, used guitar tuners, nuts and bolts, guitar strings, and some glue (see page 9).

We played with those guitars. At first I tried playing melodies on the high string while letting the other two strings function as drones, like a dulcimer. Later I learned that cigar box guitars in open tuning (tuned to a chord) are nicely suited to playing with a slide, so I tried that too.

Mostly, I enjoyed the building process. I liked it so much that I started a third guitar. This one would use a $3 piezo buzzer as a simple pickup. When I finished that guitar, I was anxious to plug it into a Dwarf amplifier I'd had around and see if it actually made noise.

It made noise. The minute I heard the roar from that tiny instrument I'd cobbled together myself out of leftovers, I burst out laughing. It seemed crazy; too good to be true.

I built another cigar box guitar after that, and then another, trying slightly different approaches with each one to solve problems I'd encountered in the construction of the others, to see if I could refine my building techniques, and in one case, adding a fourth string.

I stopped for a while at five guitars. After all, I could only play one guitar at a time (and not that well!). I didn't want to sell them or give them away. How many more could I build? So I set cigar box guitars aside for a while, though I continued to stop by cigar stores to collect empty boxes and tinker with the instruments I had made.

On a weekend getaway one winter, I took the fork of a branch and I whittled a little heart for my wife. It turned out nicely. She was touched. For Valentine's Day she got me two small books about whittling. Such a romantic! One of the books, called *The Little Book of Whittling*, impressed me. A small book, to be sure, but with clean photography, clear instructions, and a warm, first-person approach.

On my day off one Monday, I returned to the book for another look. This time I noticed a brief message on the publisher's page, something along the lines of, "if you have an idea for a woodworking book we want to hear about it—send us a letter."

On a whim I decided to send Fox Chapel Publishing an email with some pictures of the guitars I'd built. I also sent along a link to my newsletter archive so they could see samples of my writing. I sent this "message in a bottle" off to Peg Couch, the acquisition editor at Fox Chapel, and went about my business.

I arrived at work the next morning to a waiting voicemail. Peg wanted to discuss my book idea.

That was fast! It turned out that Peg had decided only the day before to pursue the very same idea. Peg's husband, Mike, a guitarist, owned a couple of cigar box guitars and had become a fan. He had been encouraging her to consider a book on the subject.

Several conversations later, my modest idea for a simple how-to project had grown into a concept for a book that would contain not only three illustrated "how-to build" projects, but also a photo gallery of different instruments and profiles of people who build and play cigar box guitars.

I was soon to discover that, in the few years since I had first looked into the subject, a huge, vibrant, international cigar box guitar community had blossomed, and that literally thousands of builders were now busily interacting across Web sites, blogs, social networking sites, eBay, YouTube, and even at festivals around the country.

In short, my work was cut out for me.

My journey began in spring 2010, with an eye-opening trip south down Kedzie Avenue in Chicago to meet Diane Sutliff, my first interviewee. In June 2010, I journeyed to Huntsville, Alabama, to attend the Sixth Annual

---

## IT MADE NOISE. THE MINUTE I HEARD THE ROAR FROM THAT TINY INSTRUMENT I'D COBBLED TOGETHER MYSELF OUT OF LEFTOVERS, I BURST OUT LAUGHING. IT SEEMED CRAZY; TOO GOOD TO BE TRUE.

---

Cigar Box Guitar Extravaganza. I talked to some people, did a few portraits, and spent the bulk of one day just photographing antique cigar box guitars, fiddles, and ukuleles, some of them dating back to the 19th century. I enjoyed two evenings of cigar box guitar music, learned a lot about a lot of things (including the amazing diddley bow), and even made some new friends.

The following August, I had the pleasure of attending a cigar box guitar festival hosted by Shane Speal in York, Pennsylvania. Again, I got to listen to some inspired music, talk to some fascinating people, and take pictures of dozens of instruments—most of them cigar-box based, but no two alike.

# INTRODUCTION TO
# CIGAR BOX GUITARS
## -OR-
# HOW I LEARNED TO STOP WORRYING
# AND MAKE SOME NOISE.
### (with apologies to Stanley Kubrick)

Welcome to the world of the Cigar Box Guitar. If you're new to it, let me start by telling you the Golden Rule of building cigar box guitars: There are no rules—there is **no one right way** to build a cigar box guitar. If you plug into the vast, supportive community of builders, you'll hear this again and again.

That said, it still is useful to familiarize yourself with some basic concepts (and I'll go over some of those) because they will increase the odds that you'll be able to produce pleasant sounds with the cigar box guitar(s) that you build.

Yes, I do predict that you will successfully build at least one cigar box guitar—in fact, that you'll probably build several.

## THE DANIEL BOONE APPROACH TO CIGAR BOX GUITARS

Someone once asked American frontiersman Daniel Boone if he'd ever been lost.

He pondered that for a bit, then responded: "I can't say as I was ever lost, but I was a might bewildered once for three days."

Borrowing from Uncle Daniel, I will tell you that I can't say as I've ever made a mistake building a cigar box guitar. I will say I've had plenty of **unexpected outcomes that inspired improvisation**, but mistakes? Naw. I will not stretch the truth—occasionally improvisation has meant deciding that I've invented a new way to produce kindling for our woodstove—but with the costs involved (I get cigar boxes from local cigar stores for $0–$2 and use primarily

"found" wood for the necks), I just chalk those happenings up to experience.

In my cigar box guitar-building experience, I have learned to eliminate the word "mistake" from my vocabulary. If cigar box guitar building and/or playing interests you at all, the only serious mistake you can make is not giving it a try.

This book is designed to get you started with useful concepts and background, not to tell you what to do. I've never built the same cigar box guitar twice, and I'm not sure I could. I build cigar box guitars because it pleases me to solve the problems inherent in building a unique guitar, and because it pleases me to play them.

# LEWIS AND CLARK
## AND WHAT THIS BOOK IS DESIGNED TO PROVIDE YOU

But—my book also has a broader mission than just the building of cigar box guitars.

My aim in writing this book—and what I am hoping that you will get from it—is to model it after the exploration in 1804–6 of the Louisiana Territory by explorers Meriwether Lewis and William Clark.

Back in 1804, Lewis and Clark were sent out to explore and map the Louisiana Territory that President Thomas Jefferson had purchased from Napoleon the previous year. They spent two years traveling, charting, and learning about the new lands.

As their epic adventure drew to a close, they retraced their steps along the Missouri eastward to their starting point in Saint Louis. Along the way, they encountered clusters of would-be settlers streaming westward into the new territory, following in their footsteps.

And, as Lewis and Clark crossed paths with these groups, they let the settlers make copies of the maps that they had drawn, and they shared information with the new settlers about things they had learned about the new lands from their explorations.

In the spirit of Lewis and Clark, this book—especially in the how-to sections—is designed to share with you my experiences in exploring the exciting new territory of building cigar box guitars. More than just showing you how I made several cigar box guitars, the book also tells (and shows) things I have seen, places I have been, and people who I have met as I have explored this new land.

My journey for this book has taken me from Huntsville, Alabama, to York, Pennsylvania, to Kansas City, Missouri, and to points in between—including that town that is the end of so many blues trails, Chicago, Illinois. I've interviewed builders and players from Memphis to Montreal; making this book has opened my world in new ways.

Here are a few of the things that you will see and people you will meet on our Lewis and Clark–style tour of the new world of Cigar Box Guitars:

- A guitar concepts primer, so you'll know which end is which (page 24).

- Detailed instructions for winding your own magnetic pickups by David "One String Willie" Williams (page 210).

- *Hundreds* of detailed gallery photos of dozens of hand-built cigar box guitars, old and new (pages 56, 72, 103, 126, and 186).

- Instructions for building a simple fretless guitar (page 36), a fretted acoustic/electric guitar (page 80), and a six-string electric guitar (page 152).

- Comments from "detritomusicologist" Bill Jehle, author of the world's first history of the cigar box guitar: *One Man's Trash* (page 66).

- A conversation with Shane Speal, "Self-Proclaimed King of the Cigar Box Guitar" (page 32). The King will also introduce us to the "Godfather of the Cigar Box Guitar," Dennis "Boz" Bostwick (page 112).

- An interview with Ted Crocker, the man who built an electric guitar, very much in the DIY spirit, that became a movie star (page 116).

- Interviews with over a dozen of the builders, players, movers, and shakers in the vibrant, North American cigar box guitar community.

- Comments and thoughts from some of the thousands of members on cigar box guitar forums about the cigar box guitar movement.

# DISCOVERING NEW FRIENDS AND OLD KIN

As you read this book, you'll discover that the process of research and writing it has been a deeply personal journey for me. Not only have I learned about the making of cigar box guitars and their history, I have made many new friends—and even discovered long-lost kin.

One of the new friends is Bill Jehle, whom I have profiled in the book. In the spirit of generosity and turnaround-is-fair-play that permeates the cigar box guitar community, Bill agreed to share these observations about me and about cigar box guitars:

## Who is David Sutton?

BY WILLIAM J. JEHLE

That's what I wanted to know. I'd been working on *One Man's Trash: A History of the Cigar Box Guitar* for four years when I learned David Sutton was also working on a book about cigar box guitars. I was struck with the feeling that many guitarists know: "so this is the *other* guitar player who I have to out-play."

I brushed that feeling away just as I have brushed aside my factory-made guitars. I soon learned that Sutton is a remarkable photographer and gifted writer, as well as a kindred spirit. As the fates had it, Sutton picks up the history of the cigar box guitar where I leave off in my own work. Whereas I was interested in the history of the cigar box guitar, Sutton was keenly interested in what is happening in the here and now. Sharing our all-too-similar life experiences with each other, we quickly became good friends. It was clear to me that he and I were two sides of the same coin.

In my own work, I was unable to ask the cigar box guitar makers from over a century ago about their motivation, let alone hear the instruments played by their original owners. Sutton, on the other hand, has ample opportunity to interview and record the modern maker and player. He was able to probe the motivation behind building, and what it means to be a cigar box guitarist.

What leads people to make cigar box guitars, banjos, fiddles, ukuleles, and other instruments in the first place? Whether obstacles like poverty or simply a dissatisfaction with commercially made instruments provide the motivation, both the building and playing of an instrument made from a cigar box can provide an education, entertainment, and community.

So, what is the cigar box guitar revolution, and why is it a revolution? Calling it a revolution implies that there is a struggle against some status quo, that something is being challenged. The cigar box guitar subverts the mainstream: the slick, commercially produced music and musical instruments of the masses.

In a conscious shift away from the "machines of music," we're replacing the slick with the homemade, the crude, and the basic, and becoming producers rather than consumers.

In the end, though, I think most of us involved have the same motivation for building and playing cigar box guitars that John Lee Hooker offers up in "Boogie Chillen":

> It's in him, and it got to come out
> And it felt so good.

*William J Jehle*
*Detritomusicologist*

# DISCOVERING OLD KIN

In addition to new friends like Bill Jehle, my travels on the cigar box guitar path also led me to the rediscovery of old kin.

Among other treasures, William J. Jehle's book, *One Man's Trash*, offers an impressive compilation of historical newspaper mentions of cigar box guitars. When I read Bill's book, I paused a long while to ponder the implications of finding my own ancestry in its pages. The following clip appears on page 161, with the dateline "Logansport Indiana":

As it turns out, Elsie Streeter, the conductor of this homemade instrument orchestra, was my great aunt, my mother's Aunt Elsie.

Bessie Wininger gets singled out because of her talent for braying like a mule—a talent my grandfather also possessed. Maybe she learned it from him. Maybe Galveston, Indiana, was just a hotbed of mule imitators. Who knows? Bessie Wininger's brother Willam, whom everyone called Bid, would grow up and marry Elsie's sister, becoming my mother's Uncle Bid. I had the great pleasure of knowing Uncle Bid because the retired telegraph operator had the grace to live a hundred years, well into my young adulthood. The name Rodibaugh even strikes me as familiar, if not familial. I'm pretty certain my grandparents played cards with the Rodibaughs.

What are the odds? Unknown to one another, two twenty-first century men set out to write books about a musical instrument originating in the 19th century. One writes about the past, one about the present, and in the process they meet and form a connection—only to discover that the connection runs deeper than either could have known. Bill Jehle's sifting turned up a connection to this subject I had sensed but could not fully know.

But there it is, folks. My relatives in Bill Jehle's cigar box guitar book.

## Church Members Hold Picnic

The members of the M. E. choir enjoyed a social evening at the church Tuesday evening. Music was furnished by the Galveston orchestra composed of cigar box fiddles, sliding trombones, gourd cornets, tin flutes and fifes, paste board cellos, jews harps and other musical instruments too numerous to mention. The stunts performed by each one afforded a great deal of fun. It certainly was amusing to hear Bessie Wininger bray like a mule, Lee Logan to sing "K-K-Katy," Elsie and Ada Rodibaugh play a piano solo, Vesper Jones cackle like a hen, Mildred Wood bark like a dog, Vergil Barnhart meow like a cat, Margaret Kitchell and Elizabeth Beeson play a piona duet, Beulah Clearwater give a reading and to see Elsie Streeter lead the orchestra, and Rev. Sanks to try to repeat the Twenty Third Psalm. Ice cream and cake were served. The eveing was ended in a big sing with Rev. Sanks at the piano.

## YOUR TURN

Now it is your turn to head out on your personal cigar box guitar path and discover what is out there for you.

My aim for this book is to share with you the fun, friends, and valuable lessons that I have learned—and to help you be ready to explore this exciting new world on your own.

Bon voyage! Don't forget to send a postcard...

# INTRODUCTION TO
# GUITAR PARTS AND CONCEPTS

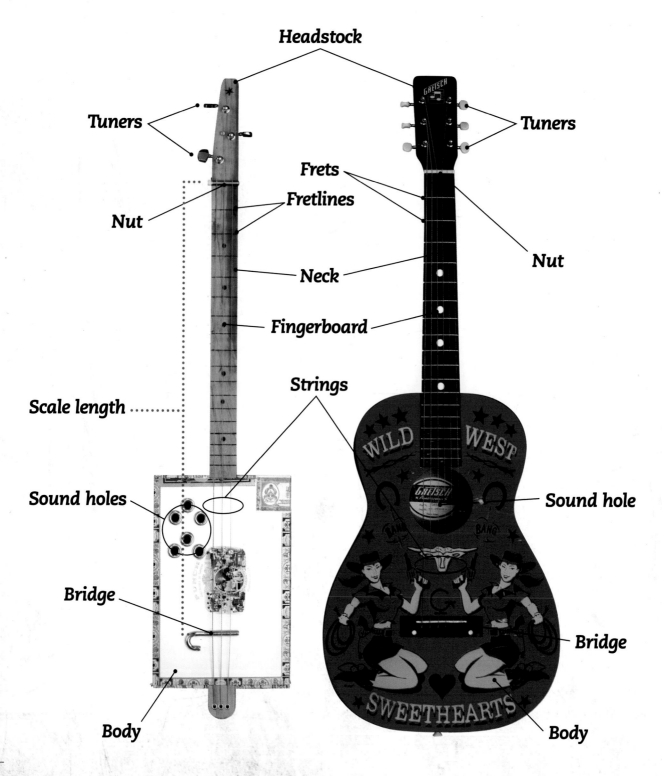

Headstock

Tuners

Tuners

Frets

Fretlines

Nut

Nut

Neck

Fingerboard

Strings

Scale length

Sound holes

Sound hole

Bridge

Bridge

Body

Body

# BODY

The guitar body is that big, wooden box, often hourglass shaped, which makes up the bulk of the instrument. The hollow box is constructed from thin wood, most often spruce or cedar. It's a fancy resonating chamber, that is, an air-filled chamber that vibrates and amplifies the sound waves produced by a vibrating string.

The top of the guitar body (the board with the hole) is often called the soundboard.

In cigar box guitar building, the guitar body usually consists of a wooden cigar box.

As luck would have it, cigar boxes are most often constructed out of cedar, either solid or thin plywood, just like most guitars. The box top acts as the soundboard, and the place where the cigars used to be becomes that air-filled resonating chamber. Some builders prefer to use the box bottom for the soundboard, because the bottom is often thinner than the top. Either works. The side where you decide to mount the strings and create a sound hole will be your top.

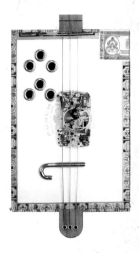

# SOUND HOLE

The sound hole or holes let all of that vibrating air inside the box vibrate the air outside the box by focusing the vibrations and projecting them forward, toward the listener. The sound hole can be any shape—in guitars, the holes are most often round, but occasionally they're shaped like a violin's f-hole. In cigar box guitars, it's all up to you—you can opt for several smaller holes,

more than one large hole, one or two f-holes, or any shape that pleases you and you're able to cut in the box top. Think about where you're putting the hole, though—I got too creative on one build and ended up with a sound hole that's largely covered by my right hand when I play. As Homer Simpson would say, "D'oh!"

# NECK

The neck is the part of the guitar that sticks out from the body and ends with the headstock, where the tuners usually live. Guitar builders favor strong, stable hardwoods, like maple or mahogany, for guitar necks. Depending on the number of strings and their material, the wood of the guitar neck can be under a tremendous amount of pressure. This pressure can quickly result in warping or bowing of the neck.

Most manufacturers of six-string guitars compensate by setting a steel truss rod into a channel in the neck beneath the fingerboard. Adjustable truss rods have threaded rods going through them and an exposed adjuster that can

be turned with an Allen wrench to force the neck back to neutral if it starts to bow.

Most cigar box guitar builders I've talked to don't incorporate that degree of sophistication into their necks. Two, three, or four strings put far less pressure on the wood than six. You can further reduce the pressure by using lighter steel or nylon strings, and/or shortening the scale.

Shortening helps in two ways. Shorter strings require less tension to make the notes they're called upon to make, and the shorter lengths of wood used for shorter necks are less susceptible to warping.

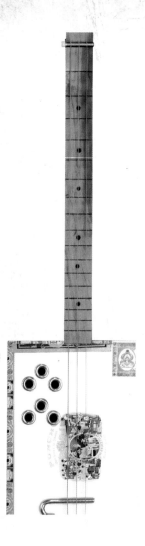

# SCALE LENGTH

The scale length refers to the sounding length of the strings, or that section of the strings that vibrates when strummed or plucked. The scale length is *physically* defined at the top end by the nut, and at the bottom end by the bridge.

Most common guitars have scale lengths somewhere between 24" and 26" (610 and 660mm). Many electric guitars use a 24½" or 25½" (622 or 648mm) scale. There's a three-way variable relationship between scale length, string gauge, and string tension. You can put the same gauge string on guitars with two different scale lengths and tune those two strings to produce the same note on both guitars. The string on the guitar with the longer scale will have higher string tension; it'll feel stiffer.

The frets or fret position markers will be closer together with a shorter scale than with a longer scale. This can be an advantage for playing chords—your fingers don't have to cover so much ground. A longer scale is advantageous if you're playing slide because you get a slightly greater margin of error in terms of placing the slide to hit the note you want. This is one of the reasons it's not uncommon to see a fretless bass guitar or contrabass, with a scale length of 34" (865mm) (Fender P. Bass) or 43" (1092mm) (upright contrabass). A millimeter's difference won't have the same impact on pitch as it would on, say, a mandolin with a 14" (356mm) scale.

Back to cigar box guitars! I've seen cigar box guitars with scale lengths from 15" to 26" (381 to 660mm). Once again, there's no right answer, and isn't that liberating? If you're thinking about slide playing, go with the longer scale. You'll have a better time hitting the notes and the stiffer strings will help keep your slide from banging into the fretboard. If you're thinking more in terms of a strummer with frets, you can lean toward the shorter scales. My best advice? Make several of each. See what you like.

# FINGERBOARD

### To fret...

The fingerboard is where human fingers interface with guitar to adjust the pitch of the vibrating strings. If the instrument has frets (those metal strips embedded at ever-closer intervals crosswise to the fingerboard) they're found here, set into the fingerboard.

Frets act as proxy nuts in that they temporarily re-define the top end of the scale. Frets become the top-end termination points for the vibrating portion of the strings. See? This normally occurs when you use your fingertip to press a string down against the fingerboard, just behind a fret.

The spacing of the frets, well, it's a bit arcane. Bill Jehle can tell you all about this with ease *and* alacrity—but never having been what you'd call a whiz at math, I have to look the details up and scratch my head a bit. I know that the twelfth fret represents the half-way point between the nut and the bridge, and that when you fret a guitar string at the twelfth fret and pluck you should hear a note one octave above the note the string sounds when plucked unfretted, or open. If you don't, then the bridge needs to be repositioned just a bit until you do. This is a critical part of guitar set-up.

Relax. I'm not going to ask you to do any math. If you want to, you certainly may; that's up to you. The method I use in this book is to copy the work that others have already done for me.

### ...or Not to Fret

If you, like Kevin Kraft (page 106), crave that flowing, silky-smooth sound you've heard Bonnie Raitt, Taj Majal, Johnny Winter, or Duane Allman produce, you might just want to learn to play with a slide.

In slide playing, the slide goes in or on the hand you finger the neck with, often over one of the fingers of that hand, and acts as a floating nut, becoming the part that temporarily redefines the top end of the scale, but this time on an unbroken continuum. In other words, the slide becomes a movable top-end termination point for the vibrating portion of the strings, and you can move the slide to produce a flowing, silky-smooth continuum of pitch, the pitch rising and falling according the length of the portion of string that's being allowed to vibrate. Not only can you slide from note to note; you can create a haunting vibrato along the way.

Guitar slides—typically a heavy, tubular piece made from metal, glass, or ceramic, and sometimes the back of a knife blade or neck of a bottle, can be any smooth, straight, solid, preferably heavy object that will fit in your hand and make clean, perpendicular contact with the strings. There's a minor myth around the now-antique Coricidin pill bottle (Duane Allman used one); other players find the bottle too light to manage.

Though you can use a slide on a fretted guitar set up for playing chords or notes, you can also build a guitar without frets, designed for slide play. Since you're making your own guitars, and since you'll probably make more than one, and since they cost you next to nothing, you can make a small arsenal of guitars, each tailored to a specific purpose.

Chicago slide guitar legend Jon Spiegel has set up one of his six-string electric guitars specifically for slide play and has others set up for playing chords.

What's the difference?

Playing with frets, many players want the strings positioned as close to the frets as they can be placed without creating a buzz when they vibrate. This makes them easy to press down far enough to get a clean note.

Spiegel outfits the slide guitar he plays with heavier strings. This enables him to make firm slide-to-string contact without pressing the strings all the way into the guitars frets, which would punctuate that sliding sound with annoying little stops.

Because the strings are heavier, he can use three plain strings and three wound strings, giving him one more plain (unwound) string than one normally sees on a six-string guitar. Normally, the heavier four strings are all wound strings. Not only do wound strings create a bit more friction, they tend to make a "zhoop zhoop" sound, like walking in corduroys, when your slide or fingers slide along their length. Plain strings don't give you that.

# STRINGS

This is where the action is—that magical point of contact between player and stringed instrument. The human player touches the string and the string responds by vibrating the air around it, which our ears and brain understand as sound.

The most elemental version of a stringed instrument is the diddley bow (known in technical circles as a monochord zither), a single string stretched taut between two points and plucked or struck with some sort of striker. Richard Johnston (page 138) said he'd read that the archers of old were the original diddley bow players, coaxing music out of their weapons during slow periods in the killing.

Commercial guitar strings usually come in sets of six different gauges and may be made of steel, nylon, bronze, silk wrapped around steel together with a bronze wind over that, or any of a number of other exotic materials.

Heavier strings for the deeper notes typically use wound strings utilizing a lighter-gauge wire wound around a heavier-gauge wire. This process gives the string more weight—meaning a deeper sound—while maintaining its flexibility.

Strings for electric guitars using magnetic coil pickups (pups) must be made from ferrous metal in order to disturb the pickup's magnetic field enough to create an electrical signal.

# HEADSTOCK AND THE STRING BREAK CONUNDRUM

Once you start building cigar box guitars, you'll become familiar with the "headstock/tuner problem" and you can have a lot of fun figuring out solutions to this little conundrum, or just poking around the web seeing how many different ways other builders have found to manage it.

Standard guitar tuners are too long for the most basic cigar box guitars! We use them anyway! Our most common neck currency in the CBG world is the "one-by" as in one-by-two (1x2). Kiln-dried, dimensioned stock is neither "one" nor "by two," but that's what they call it because that's what it measured before they stuck it into the kiln. Dried, it's roughly ¾" by roughly 1½" (19 x 38mm).

The problem lies with the ¾" (19mm). That thickness feels great in the hand and makes a nearly ideal neck. Hacking away ¼" (6mm) from the upper side of the headstock may make room for the strings to "break" at the nut, but a standard guitar tuner's too long, and the hole for the string ends up at or above the level of the nut. That means the string doesn't break at the nut, so it's not held securely enough in the groove. That makes the string prone to popping out and/or buzzing when you play.

Cigar box guitar builders seem to take quite a bit of pleasure in re-inventing this particular wheel—I know I certainly do. We want to solve the same problems the "big boys" solve, but in the spirit of keeping it cheap and simple.

Commercially manufactured guitars generally have a fretboard—a separate piece of about ³⁄₁₆" (5mm)-thick wood glued onto the flat side of the neck. This raises the strings a bit above the headstock. In addition to that, they generally solve the problem one of two ways: by using a scarf joint to angle the headstock back (most acoustics), or by adding string trees to pull the longest strings down closer to the headstock (many Fender-style electrics).

On my first two guitars, I compensated by winding a lot of each string around the tuner post so that the string left the post at the lowest possible point. That may not be enough, so a lot of cigar box guitar builders do as I did on my first two guitars and invent their own string trees.

On my third guitar, I started with a thicker piece of wood and cut it down from the back, leaving an angled headstock. This solution can look like you've made a scarf joint, but it will never be as strong because the angle leaves some very short wood grain right at the point of greatest stress. It's true the three or four strings you put on your CBG won't be loading the neck with a hundred fifty to two hundred pounds of pressure like six strings would, but that angle may still be vulnerable.

For my fourth guitar, I glued a short piece of 1x2 to the back of the neck piece so it extended 5" or 6" (127 or 152mm), then I smoothed out the joint. That dropped the tuners down a whopping ¾" (19mm). It certainly gave me the string break

I was looking for, and speaking of break, the headstock snapped off at the joint while I was shaping it. The ensuing repair job has held up respectably well, but I haven't gone back to that particular solution.

Here are some other solutions I've seen used or used myself:

- Use ukulele tuners (they're shorter!)
- Add a ¼" (6mm)-thick piece of plywood or other wood to the back of the headstock
- Glue a ³⁄₁₆" or ¼" (5 or 6mm) fretless fretboard to the front of the neck. You don't need to put frets in it—it'll serve the purpose of getting the strings high enough above the headstock to create a respectable break angle at the nut.
- Use pan-head screws as simple string trees
- Make a string tree out of brass or wood

- Use tuners designed for a slotted headstock like you see on many classical guitars (as I did in the second build in this book)
- Go for the glory: make a simple jig and start cutting and gluing your own scarf joints

If you look closely at a modern Telecaster or Stratocaster, you'll notice a string tree holding down just the two longest strings. Both these designs use an in-line headstock rather than an angled headstock. Part of the thickness is routed away and some elevation is achieved with the addition of a fretboard, but the two longest strings still need some help. Why just those two? Geometry. If you turn one of these guitars sideways and look at the headstock from the side, you'll notice that the angle at which the strings leave the nut for the tuners DEcreases as the distance between the nut and the tuners INcreases. The two strings routed to the tuners most distant from the nut therefore require a string tree to achieve a solid, effective break angle.

# THE NUT

The nut defines the top end of the scale. This is the top-end termination point for the vibrating portion of the strings. The slots in the nut act as spacers and guides for the strings, which keeps them from sliding side to side. The nut also holds the strings at a useful height above the fretboard—higher for fretless instruments played with a slide; lower for fretted instruments. As with the bridge, commercial builders usually fabricate the nut from some dense material like bone or brass. We might use an old bolt.

# BRIDGE (AND SADDLE)

The bridge defines the bottom end of the scale. It's the bottom-end termination point for the vibrating portion of the strings. The strings pull taut over the bridge, allowing it to transfer vibrations from the strings to the soundboard. Denser materials do a better job of this, which is why bridges are often made of bone or high-density composites. With conventional acoustic guitars, the bridge normally rests atop a piece of hardwood called the saddle, which not only keeps the bridge in place, but provides a nice, thick anchor for the stationary end of the strings.

In cigar box guitar building, the bridge can be anything that will keep the strings a short distance above the soundboard and cause a "break" or bend in the strings. The bridge often has grooves that help to keep the strings separated by the correct distance. Threaded rods or bolts come to mind.

# TOOL TIPS

Before you jump in to the projects, read through this bit about tools—it will save you a lot of time in the long run!

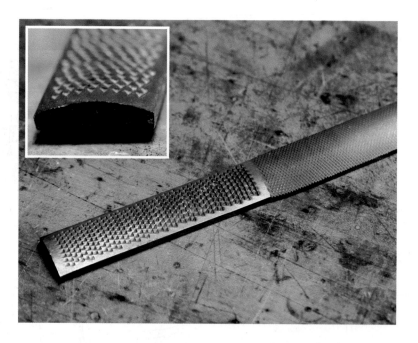

Four-in-hand rasp/file combo.

Get a **four-in-hand rasp/file combo**—one of the most useful tools around. It has four different cutting surfaces in one palm-sized package: two rasps and two coarse files, one each flat and curved. It's great to be able to go from cutting and shaping to smoothing with just a flip of the wrist, and you can use a four-in-hand to cut, shape, smooth, and adjust.

Files are edge tools. That is, they have cutting edges just like knives, chisels, and planes. If you want to keep your files in top working order, handle them with the same respect you would a fine knife. Don't throw your files in a drawer, clanking against each other—it dulls them. Instead, wrap them up in an old pantleg or a towel.

**Keep your edge tools super sharp.** Not only does it make for a more gratifying building experience—sharp tools are safer than dull tools. Initial sharpening takes some time and some getting used to, but once you've got a good edge on your chisel, knife, or plane, you'll seldom need to do more than touch it up on a strop.

Whenever I can, I prefer to **use non-powered hand tools.** The kind of tools our granddads used made very little noise and next to no airborne dust. They're more forgiving when it comes to slips—it's pretty hard to hack off a digit with a handsaw, and it's hard to avoid it with a table saw or circular saw. Human-powered hand tools are better for the greater environment and also make for a more pleasing local environment, namely, your shop. If your aim is to manufacture on a larger scale, then power tools and dust collection systems will be on your shopping list. If you're building for pleasure, though, keep in mind that power tools too often become obstacles to that pleasure. Designed for production work, power tools often take longer to set up than it would take to perform the same operation with a hand tool. Have you ever tried to do something on a computer and, fifteen minutes into the task, realized you could have picked up a pencil or a telephone and been done with it? It's like that. If it's a choice between designing and building a jig so that I can safely make a cut with my table saw and grabbing a chisel and mallet, I'll go for the chisel.

In many cases, **a number of different tools could be used to accomplish the same task.** I'll make an effort to talk about alternatives as we go. Part of the thrill of building cigar box guitars stems from the "something from nothing" quality of building an instrument capable of producing serious music out of odds and ends you already own. In a similar spirit, please don't hamstring your production by thinking you don't have the right tool for the job and you need to BUY something. Be flexible—rather than running out to the tool depot every time you come upon an obstacle, stop and think for a bit. There's probably another way. There are many roads to Rome—whenever you can, use what you have.

I prefer **marking knives** over pencils for most marking jobs. Because it makes a finer line, the marking knife is more accurate. While a pencil gives you a visual reference, the marking knife gives you a physical reference in addition to the visual. This can be very helpful, as you'll see, for lining up a cutting tool, such as a saw or a chisel. The downside is that mistakes don't erase as readily as pencil marks. In general, I don't mind builder's markings or tool impressions making an appearance in the final product. I like the way it connects product to process—a connection I think is too often missing in our highly refined, ultra-polished, commercially manufactured goods.

**Learn to use hand planes and their cousins, spokeshaves.** Start small with a block plane or a smoother and learn how to take one apart, sharpen the iron, assemble, adjust, and cut with it. Shaving off a thin, wavy ribbon of wood and feeling the perfectly flat, glass-smooth surface left behind has to be one of woodworking's most satisfying experiences.

**Magnets.** I have a weird assortment of magnets around my shop, which I find useful in all kinds of applications. Rare earth or neodymium magnets are incredibly powerful and quite versatile.

Marking knife.

Hand plane.

**Measure twice, cut once.** My grandfather Sutton taught building trades. When he'd get a green group of youngsters he'd instruct them, "Now, when you get ready to cut a board, be sure to err on the side of cutting it too short. You can always stick a piece of wood back on, but it's harder than the devil to trim a piece that's too long." That invariably got their attention and caused them to engage their brains, which was his objective. I think.

# SHANE SPEAL
## CONVERSATION WITH THE KING

*Shane Speal, self-proclaimed King of the Cigar Box Guitar, is a big player in the handmade music movement. The site he started, Cigar Box Nation, has been a gathering place for CBG builders since the nineties. Photos and videos of Shane Speal initially gave me the impression of a lumbering, somewhat intimidating fellow, whose five-o'clock shadow probably came in at noon.*

*In person, the impression runs more along the lines of a super-charged Charlie Brown—amicable, energetic, and inspiring. Shane and I spoke at the First Capitol Brewing Company in York, Pennsylvania, the night before the big York Cigar Box Guitar Festival in August of 2010.*

*Seven Hill Stomp provided a background soundtrack, and Shane took a break halfway through our talk to sit in with them for a couple of tunes.*

**SS:** I grew up in the outskirts of Pittsburgh, in a little town called New Alexandria, Pennsylvania. I first saw KISS on TV—I think it was the *Midnight Special*—when I was five years old, and that was it. Ever since I saw KISS on TV I wanted to be a musician.

When I turned eight my dad bought me my first guitar. I had to make sure it had two "points" on it—two cutaways—because that's what Gene Simmons' guitar had. I didn't know at the time Simmons played bass.

I wanted to be KISS. I still do.

I grew up, and as I grew up I played in heavy metal bands. In the eighties, during high school, I ended up switching to bass and playing a lot of Rush, classic rock, Led Zeppelin, things like that. In the late eighties, I even joined a death/thrash band for a while, playing bass for them. That was the Mothers of Madness. We never made it out of the garage.

Soon after that I went to college, and that's where I discovered the blues. Any time someone discovers the blues they go through that "natural" progression. You find Jimi Hendrix and Jimmy Paige and those guys. GREAT! Who influenced them? You take one step back and you get Muddy Waters and Hound Dog Taylor. Who influenced them? You take one step back and you get Robert Johnson and Blind Willy Johnson.

**Shane Speal** creates a little "back porch mojo" with a Kurt Schoen four-string resonator CBG.

I asked the question, who came before them? At the time I couldn't find out what came before them. Then I discovered the cigar box guitar. To me, it was that One Step Deeper than the delta blues.

## DS: Can you describe that discovery?

**SS:** A friend of mine gave me a bunch of his dad's old *Guitar Player* magazines. There was an article from 1976. Some guy made a really crude version of the two-string cigar box guitar Carl Perkins started out on.

I went nuts.

I built my first one on July 3, 1993. It was a three string. As soon as I built it, I could play it. I had been struggling with six-string slide, trying to get that Taj Mahal alternating thumb thing going. It was so tough! As soon as I picked up the cigar box guitar I felt like freakin' Yngwie Malmsteen*. I mean, I was just burning on the thing.

I knew that was mine. It was an instrument nobody else had. It was one thing that set me apart from everyone else, because on a regular guitar I sounded like a poor man's Jimi Hendrix, and who wants to be that?

# IT WAS LIKE PEELING BACK THE LAYERS AND GETTING TO THE ESSENCE.

**DS: Tell me about building that first guitar.**

**SS:** I went out to my dad's farm. My dad has a little 110-acre farm out in Saltsburg, Pennsylvania. I went out and pulled a board out of his barn; I guess it was a big, old, oak timber. I didn't know what I was doing. When I tried to cut it, the saw blade was burning the wood and everything else—so it was this massive neck on a cardboard Swisher Sweets box.

I put three old guitar strings on there and just beat the hell out of it.

**DS: But you found the sound gratifying right away?**

**SS:** ABSOLUTELY. Absolutely. Right away. It was MINE. It was my sound, my guitar.

**DS: You said that you kept going after deeper influences. What is it about you that made you want to keep going backward like that?**

**Shane Speal and Shane Speal II** performing at the 2010 York, PA, Cigar Box Guitar Festival.

**SS:** I love the gritty old sound. Before I made the cigar box guitar, I was playing a beat-to-hell old Stella with action about ¾" at the 12th fret. They were the best guitars in the world as far as acoustics, and I just wanted that sound. It was like peeling back the layers and getting to the essence.

**DS: How did your Web site get started?**

**SS:** Do you remember Geocities, those homemade websites? I made a one-page Geocities. I am not one to show people how to do things; I'm not a teacher. In just very simple terms, I put up one page on how to build a cigar box guitar. I put it up for free. Back then everybody wanted to charge for something. I just put it up for free.

There was just one picture of the guitar I built and easy steps on how to do it. People started emailing me. They were stumbling upon it and they kept asking me the same questions. So after about eight months of this I started a Yahoo chat-room—I figured I'd use that to answer all the questions at once. From there—that grew into 3,000 members.

**DS: Your mission is to show the world the cigar box guitar. You're not that into the actual building; you like to keep your guitars very crude. Is it the guitar itself that you're showing the world?**

**SS:** What I'm showing the world is, anybody can be a guitarist. Anybody can be a musician.

People always say things like, I'm going to write a book, and they never write the book. What I'm saying is, it's time to write the damn book. It's time to build the guitar and get out there and play. You know what? A cheap home recording unit today is better technology than the Beatles had when they recorded *Revolver*. You have it. Use it.

\*  Swedish heavy-metal guitar virtuoso, multi-instrumentalist, and pioneer of "shred" guitar.

I'm an enabler. I'm telling everyone, "Get out there and do it." I don't care how bad you sound; I don't care how good you sound. With a cigar box guitar there's no rules, so whatever you play is perfectly fine.

**DS:** Why do you think that's important?

**SS:** Because so many people are stifled in their creativity. They think "I can't sing" or … whatever.

COME ON. We're on this earth for how long? Do something beautiful while you're here. Create something great. Start a revolution! (He laughs) That's what I did!

**DS:** Tell me about the first time you had the notion that that's what you were going to do, you were going to start a revolution.

**SS:** I never thought it would be this. I just said this stuff. I remember preaching on the Internet, "This is a new thing, the cigar box guitar revolution, it's going to be huge." I had no idea; I was just saying it. But the thing is, if you lead, some people will follow.

Some of the people who followed me are the misfits of music. These guys who never got out of their living rooms, who always struggled to play guitar. I'm saying, Come on, let's do our own thing. Don't let anyone tell you you have to play like Stevie Ray, or, God help us, Eric Clapton. Get out there and just be yourself.

**DS:** With the recordings, the emphasis came around to perfection, and that there is ONE right way to make music. That's incredibly stifling.

When I interviewed Diane Sutliff (page 62), she pointed out that people think they shouldn't pick up an instrument because they're not "good enough."

**Shane Speal's Old Faithful.** Shane built this three-string in 1996 and has used it ever since.

**SS:** THAT is IT. We're destroying that rule. That is the key. We're absolutely destroying that rule. We're saying everyone can do it.

I'm looking at all the guys that are like me, you know? The "losers" in music. I don't mean "loser" in the traditional connotation, but those of us who never got the recording contract, never played at an open mic or a coffee shop, who were always too afraid.

The one person who personifies that for me was a man named Donald Bostwick (page 112). We called him Boz. Donald was dying of lung cancer and discovered the cigar box guitar. All his life he'd played, but never played for anyone. Then he started playing cigar box guitar. By the time he died I think he'd released eight albums.

He played from Michigan down to Huntsville, to West Virginia, to New Jersey, everywhere. You know what? In three years he lived out the musician's life. It was because we destroyed the rules. ■

# Build #1:
# SIMPLE FRETLESS ACOUSTIC GUITAR

## Guitar number ONE: The basics.

I'll build a fretless, acoustic, three-string CBG intended for playing with a slide or bottleneck. This guitar's pretty simple and costs almost nothing. If you have all the parts on hand, you can get it built over the course of an afternoon. Don't underestimate it though—it's a music maker capable of putting out a respectable sound!

## MATERIALS

- Wooden cigar box (square sided and paper covered)
- 1x2 (19 x 38mm), 3' (915mm) poplar or other wood—pithy pine will likely warp on you; poplar is suggested here because it's readily available and inexpensive. You can opt for harder and/or more exotic woods if you feel comfortable working with them.
- (6) Brass eyelets
- (6) Brass grommets
- ¼" (6mm) hex head bolt, 1½" (40mm) long
- ⁵⁄₁₆" (8mm) J bolt, 1½" to 2" (40 to 50mm) long (or a set screw or threaded rod—anything without a head)
- (3) Used guitar tuners
- (3) Guitar strings (E, A, D)

## TOOLS

**NECESSARY:**
- Handsaw
- Square
- Yardstick
- Pencil (or marking knife)
- Utility knife
- Phillips head screwdriver
- Drill and bits
- Clamps
- Rasp or file
- Sandpaper
- Epoxy
- Wood glue

**HELPFUL:**
- Block plane
- 2" (50mm) chisel
- Woodburner or a fine-point permanent marker
- Spokeshave
- Toothpicks

This unassuming pile of stuff will become a playable CBG with your help!

This homely gathering of tools will be all you need to construct your CBG.

# GETTING STARTED

If you'd like, you can use a razor to cut the lid off and make life a little easier (you'll reattach the lid later), or you can just work around it like I did.

Select a piece of wood for the neck. For simplicity's sake, I picked up a piece of 1x2 (19 x 38mm) poplar from the moldings section of the local hardware store. A 6' (1830mm) piece cost a little over $5 and gave me enough wood for two guitar necks. Poplar's not my first choice of woods—it's soft and may eventually bow under the pull of the strings, but it's inexpensive, generally available, and more rigid than the ubiquitous white pine you find in building centers. If you mess it up, you're out two bucks. Since this particular guitar is meant for slide playing, the bowing, if any, won't affect your playing much.

Mark off the headstock/string nut line.

Position the bridge mark about one-quarter of the way up from the bottom of the box.

# NOTCHING THE CIGAR BOX

**1** **Lay out the important neck locations.** Lay your neck board out on a work surface and measure 6" (150mm) in from one end for the headstock. Use a square to make a mark all the way across and down two sides. This is where the guitar's nut will be. The nut is the "zero" point for your scale. Measure 24½" (620mm) from the nut to locate the bridge and strike a line across that point as well.

**2** **Position the bridge.** Lay the neck on top of the box so that roughly 3" (75mm) protrudes from the tail end of the box. Slide the neck back and forth, if necessary, until the 24½" (620mm) bridge mark ends up about one-quarter of the way up from the tail end of the box (the location will vary depending on the size of your box). When you've located the bridge, make a light pencil mark on the box top where the bridge will be. Mark the neck board at both ends to indicate the sides of the cigar box.

**3** **Mark the neck position.** Open the box and mark the center point on each end of the opening. Line up the center of the neck with the centers of the box sides. Mark out the width of the neck on the box sides. Flip the box over so the opening is face down; place the neck flat on its wide face next to the box and scribe the neck's thickness between the two width lines. This will be the notch you cut out.

Find and mark centerlines on the neck board and on the ends of the box.

Use the neck stock to mark the depth of the cut.

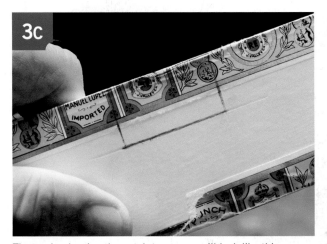

The marks showing the notch to remove will look like this.

**4** **Remove the notch and fit the neck.** Remove this rectangle of wood from both ends of the box. You can do this with a fine saw, but I prefer a sharp utility knife. The blade is thinner and a saw is likely to produce tear-out and rough edges. Cigar boxes are most commonly made of cedar plywood, which is soft and can splinter when you saw it. The utility knife gives a nice, clean cut. Cut on the insides of your lines—it's better to start with the opening a bit too small and file it open to fit. If you cut too big, then you may end up with some gaps. Keep at it until the neck fits snugly into the openings. Line up the marks on the underside of the neck with the box's edge and mark across the top of the neck on both edges of the lid. Caution: Don't force the neck into the box! It should slide in with just a little resistance. Cigar boxes weren't built to last—they can be delicate.

> "There is something about handmade instruments that whispers, 'If you want to play, you are supposed to make your own.' So I did."
>
> **—NANCY BARNES,**
> **HANDMADE MUSIC CLUBHOUSE**

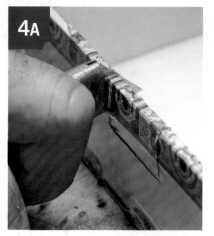

Cut out the neck slot with a utility knife.

The notch is cut out.

Rasp or file the notch for a clean, snug fit.

Here, the neck is seated, with the top of the board flush with top of the box.

Mark the board where the lid will nest into it.

**5**

Use the edge of the lid as a guide to mark the depth of wood to be removed.

**6A**

Make several saw cuts just to the desired depth.

# PREPARING THE NECK

The next several steps involve the neck; so put your cigar box safely aside somewhere. We need to reduce the thickness of the neck board in two places.

Because we want the fingerboard (the part of the neck with the frets on it) flush with the lid, we need to take the part of the neck that's under the lid down by the thickness of the lid. If the fingerboard were lower than the box top, the strings would have to be that much farther away from the neck in order to pass over the guitar's body. We want to keep the strings closer to the neck.

We'll also thin out the headstock area by about ¼" (6mm) so the guitar strings can "break" or angle down at the nut; this keeps them solidly against the nut, reducing the likelihood of string buzz.

**5** Mark the neck wood under the box lid to be removed. I use a marking knife and the box lid itself to score a line between the two box end marks. By using the box lid, you are ensuring that the depth is perfect.

**6** Remove the wood. Using a backsaw, make some cuts along the area to be removed, using the scored lines as a depth stop. At this point, I like to use a 2" (50mm) chisel to hog away the bulk of the wood, and a file to even up and finish off the bottom of the cutaway.

**6B**

Use the saw cuts and scribed line as guides to chop out waste with a chisel.

**6C**

Chisel along the length to continue to remove wood.

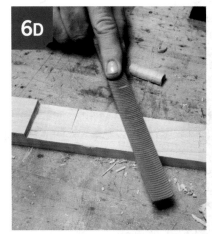

**6D**

File the cutaway area to even it up and bring it completely to the scribed line.

**7** **Test the neck fit.** Fit the neck back into the cigar box and test the fit by closing the lid. The lid should come down cleanly and nest without using any force. Make sure it's a good fit—the wood used in making cigar boxes is so thin and flexible that it's easy to distort the box if you force things into place.

**8** **Remove wood on the headstock.** The next step is to cut down the headstock area. I'm using the 5⁄16" (8mm) bolt as a guide (use whatever you want to install as the nut)—I want about a third of the bolt to rise above the fingerboard. Mark the depth, extend those lines, then use a thin saw, chisel, and file to reduce the thickness.

Fit the neck back into the box, careful to align the cut-away portion with the lid.

The neck board is seated in the box.

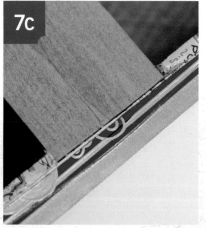

Here, you can see the nice clean fit where the lid nests into the neck.

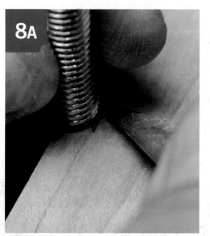

Use the nut to determine the depth of cut to make for the headstock area. We'll take away about a third of the thickness.

Mark the area to be removed for the headstock.

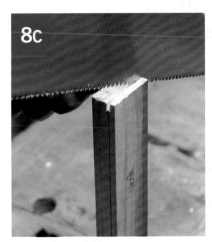

**8C**

I used a fine-toothed saw to cut away wood for the headstock. You may also use a rasp, chisel, or table saw for this operation.

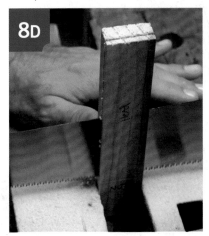

**8D**

Stop the cut just before the nut line.

**8E**

I use a large, heavy chisel and mallet to cut away the waste at the nut line. You can also use a fine-toothed saw.

**8F**

File or sand the headstock surface smooth.

# HEADS AND TAILS
## (HEADSTOCK AND TAILPIECE)

**9** **Mark the string positions.** Now it's time to position the tuners on the headstock. In order to locate the tuners, we need to know where the strings will be. Since the guitar will have three strings, we want the second string in the center of the neck. Mark the centerline, then mark ⅜" (10mm) to either side of this for the bottom and top strings. That spacing is slightly wider than a conventional guitar, but helpful when playing slide. You can experiment with spacing until you find a solution that suits your playing.

**10** **Place the tuners.** Follow the string lines down onto the headstock. I find it helpful to disassemble the tuners and lay the mounting plates on the back of the headstock. The first tuner-post should be at least 1½" (40mm) from the nut. I'll put one on each side here. Now arrange the plates so the SIDE (not the center) of the string-post-hole aligns with the string's path. The third tuner will go on the top edge, about 1½" (40mm) from the first one. Trace the mounting plates onto the headstock and set the plates aside.

**11** **Shape the headstock.** When you know where the tuners need to be, you can shape the headstock a little. I like to use a saw, four-in-hand rasp, and block plane to create the shape. Taper one side of the headstock to keep the tuners the same distance from the edge while maintaining string alignment.

**12** **Drill holes in the headstock for the tuners.** The holes have to fit the tuner bushings, which are usually ¼" (6mm). I've drilled the bushing side of the hole (on that face of the headstock) to ¼" (6mm) and the tuner side to the exact size of the tuner post. The ¼" (6mm) hole by itself would also serve just fine.

Disassemble the tuners.

Use the tuner mounting plates to locate the holes for the tuner posts. The side of the headstock will need to be angled to fit the tuners so that they're not right in line with one another.

Shape the headstock using whatever tools you like.

Drill holes for the tuning machine posts.

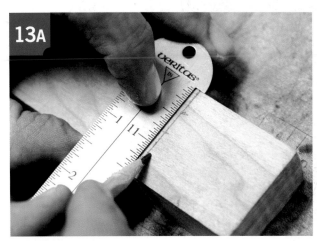

Mark off the string anchor holes ⅜" (10mm) apart on the tailpiece.

Drill holes for the string anchors large enough to accept the brass eyelets.

I used an errant cork stopper as a pattern for the tail end of my guitar. You may opt to leave it square.

**13** **Shape the tailpiece.** At the opposite end of the neck, perform a corresponding operation—lay out the string anchor holes and give some shape to the bottom end of the neck board. Drill three ³⁄₁₆" (5mm) holes about 1 ½" (40mm) from the end of the box and with the same spacing as the strings. Once again, drill the center string hole dead center and the other two ⅜" (10mm) to either side of that one. At this point, use something round (I used a cork) to lay out a curve, and then use a saw, block plane, rasp, and file to shape it to the line.

Saw away the corners and shape the tailpiece.

**14**

**15**

Epoxy the eyelets in place.

**14** **Install string eyelets.** Use a toothpick to spread a bit of epoxy around each hole and glue the eyelets into the holes. Make sure the epoxy doesn't close up the string hole—this can be tough to remove without taking out the eyelet too.

**15** **Shape the neck.** Now comes my favorite part: Shaping the neck. It's necessary to strike a balance between creating a comfortable profile and leaving as much wood as possible for strength. Some builders do no more than knock down the sharp corners with sandpaper, or round over the back corners with a rasp or a router, but I like to take it a down with a curved spokeshave. Once again, if you don't have a spokeshave, a rasp and file and/or sandpaper will do a pretty nice job.

Shape the neck. A spokeshave is ideal but not mandatory. You can also use sandpaper, a router, or a rasp and file. Just make it fit your hand without removing too much wood.

## SLIDES

So many slides, so little time!

Guitar slides come in all shapes and sizes. Starting at upper left: A glazed ceramic slide from Moonshine Guitar Slides has nice heft and stays slippery; it comes in two lengths and different diameters. The solid brass AcoustaGlide slide is marvelous—if you keep it polished. This third slide is a very heavy, short one preferred by Chicago slide master Jon Spiegel; it's actually modeled after slides cut from Harley Davidson motorcycle handlebars. The front right is an 18mm socket, favored by Shane Speal; some players prefer a deeper socket, but Speal gets a lot of mileage out of this shorty, working individual strings or all three. Lastly, a chromed metal slide. There are many more types of slides out there, made out of many different materials—and each will coax a different sound out of your guitar.

# LAYING OUT THE FRET LINES

**16** **Get a fret scale pattern.** We'll need a 24½" (620mm) (nut to bridge) guitar fret scale pattern to lay out the fret lines. There are a number of ways to get a template for a fret scale, the simplest of which is to use paper and pencil to transfer the locations from an existing guitar. You can poke around the Internet a bit and find spreadsheets—search for "fret placement calculators," "pdf fret placement templates for download," or purchase templates from lutherie suppliers.

**17** **Lay out the scale.** First, put your bolt at the bottom of the headstock. Lay the scale out with the nut line (fret #0) at the very center of the bolt and measure from there.

**18** **Mark the frets.** Using tiny pieces of double-stick carpet tape on the back of the scale to hold it in place, use a square and marking knife to make a nick in the neck at each fret location. Then, remove the template and, using a square as a guide, carry the line all the way across with a marking knife or pencil. Make a nice, deep cut. The marking knife offers a big advantage in this particular operation—instead of trying to line the square up perfectly with each mark by eye, I can feel the mark with the knife, position it in the nick I've made, and then bring the square up to the knife (instead of the other way around).

18A

Tape the fret guide in place and mark off fret lines.

18B

Scribe fret lines into fret board with a marking knife, or draw them on with a marker.

**19** **Darken the fret lines.** The next step can be done with a fine-point permanent marker, but I'm going to heat up a woodburner with a knife-blade tip and actually burn the lines in. Another alternative is scratching deeply enough with the marking knife, and then staining the neck (the stain will darken the lines). When the lines are in, I can put position markers wherever I find it helpful. A conventional six-string guitar has position markers at 3, 5, 7, 9, and 12 (sometimes 15 and 17, too), but I'm going to put my markers at 3, 5, 7, 10, 12, and 15 to reference a blues scale. I also like to add a small decorative burn on the headstock just for kicks.

I use a woodburner to darken the fret lines.

Position markers are optional on a fretless guitar like this one. If you're experienced at playing by ear, you may leave them off altogether (as well as fret lines). I moved one marker one fret so a beginning player could play a blues scale by following the dots.

Personalize your cigar box guitar by decorating the headstock, if you like.

20A

**20** **Finish the neck.** When you're happy with the shape and markings, it's time to finish the neck with some sandpaper. I like using shellac because, once dried, it's non-toxic, and I can mix it up in small batches, as I need it. It dries fast, so I can build up coats more quickly than I can with urethanes or varnish. It cleans up with alcohol rather than paint thinner, too. Note: Don't put finish on the part of the board that fits inside the box—we'll need glue to stick to that area.

Sand the neck.

# ATTACH THE TUNERS AND NUT

**21** **Install tuner bushings.** The neck is almost finished, which means we're in the home stretch. Next, we'll attach the tuners and the nut. Start by gently tapping the tuner bushings down into their holes.

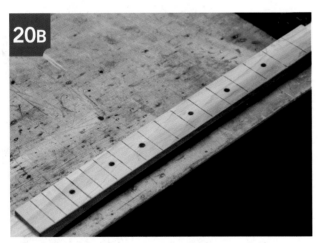

20B

It's starting to look like a guitar neck! Choose your finish and apply.

21

Tap in the press-fit tuner bushings.

**22** **Install the nut.** Next, we'll glue the guitar's nut (the bolt) into place against the headstock. I just use a drop of epoxy under the bolt to keep it steady. I think some of the purists just let the bolt float, held in place by the string tension, but I like the solid connection epoxy gives me, and I like not having to keep track of the nut (bolt?!) when I change strings.

**23** **Install the tuners.** After the epoxy sets, put the reassembled tuners into position and use their tiny screws to anchor them in place.

## ADDITIONAL TUNING SUGGESTIONS:

E   (E—B—E')

A   (A—E—A')

G   (G—D—G')

A7  (A—E—G')

G9  (G—D—A')

Use a small dab of epoxy to fix the bolt. Keep the head of the bolt pointed up so your hand doesn't run into it when you play.

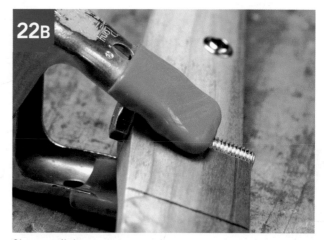

Clamp until dry.

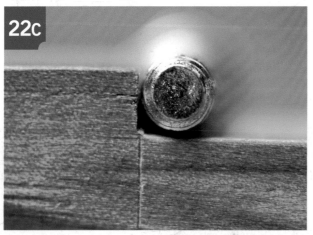

String nut in position, just high enough above the fretboard.

Mount the tuners.

# BACK TO THE BOX: SOUND HOLES

The music has to find its way out of the cigar box, so I'm going to cut some sound holes. I have a number of options here—I can cut one big hole, a series of smaller holes, all different sizes, or even "f-holes," as on violins and some guitars and mandolins. Positioning the sound hole/s offers another creative design opportunity. Keep in mind, though, that you DON'T want the sound hole to be right under your playing hand because your hand will block the sound (don't ask me how I know this). Pay attention to the placement of the neck, as well—the neck goes all the way through, so avoid putting a sound hole right where the neck will be.

**24** **Mark the sound hole locations.** I opted for a double arrow pattern of brass grommets. Position the grommets, mark their centers, then drill the sound holes out to size. As my box lid is too thick to "set" the grommets, I just glued them in place with a bit of epoxy.

When I drilled out these sound holes, I was surprised to discover that the box top was actually Masonite, rather than plywood like the sides. This was a first for me, so I was anxious to see how that would affect the sound. Fortunately, I wouldn't have to wait much longer…

Design your sound hole/s.

Mark the box for drilling the sound holes.

Here, the box lid is drilled out.

Cement the grommets in place.

# REINFORCING THE BOX

**25** **Add structural support blocks.** To give the guitar neck a nice, solid connection with the box, and to give the box more structural support, cut a couple of blocks of 1x2 poplar: one to fit in each short end of the box. The cutouts for the neck should fit smoothly—not too tight, but no wiggle room. Glue and clamp the blocks into place.

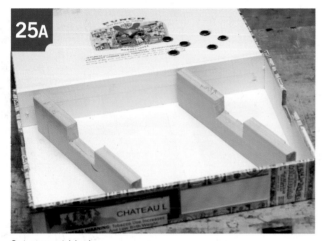

Cut support blocks.

> "Playing any instrument is an embodiment of heart, mind, soul, and whatever else is part of our makeup."
>
> **—STEVE, CIGAR BOX NATION**

Glue the supports into place with wood glue and clamp.

## 26 Glue up the guitar.
Now, we get to glue it all up and make it look like a guitar! Slide the neck into the box, checking that the marks line up with the sides of the box, and that the lid closes cleanly, without force. Make any final adjustments necessary to achieve this. When you're satisfied with the fit, spread glue along the tops of the support blocks and the cutaway portion of the guitar neck, as well as the long edges where the lid makes contact with the box. At the last minute, I decided to trim the paper covering away from the wood where the long sides make contact so I could apply glue directly to the wood (not shown). The last construction step is to close the lid and clamp it in place, then set it aside while the glue dries.

Position the neck carefully; test-fit the lid.

Put glue on the tops of the supports and neck.

Clamp down the lid.

# STRING IT UP

**27** **Install a string.** I used acoustic guitar strings in gauges .042 (E), .032 (A), and .024 (D). You may opt to use the "top" three strings instead (G, B, E) for a very different sound. Pick one string and thread it back to front through its "home" hole in the tailpiece so the string's ball-end is in the back. Because the guitar tuners I'm using are a bit long, I stretch the string up to the tuning peg, but don't put it through the hole right away. Instead, I'm going to wrap the string around the post from bottom to top as many times as will fit so that the string leaves the post at the lowest possible point, and then poke it through the anchor hole in the tuning peg.

Go get your strings!

Thread the strings in from the back.

Over-wind the string around the post so the string exits the post as low as possible.

**28** **Install the bridge.** Use the tuning machine to tighten the string, and, as it tightens, insert the J-bolt bridge under the string at the bridge position of the scale (in this case, at 24½" [620mm]). Keep tightening until the tension holds the bridge in place—just enough to make it sound like a note—and excitedly enjoy hearing your new guitar's voice for the first time.

Position the bridge (J-bolt or threaded rod) AT 24½" (620mm).

**29**

**Add the other strings.** Add the other two strings in the same way you installed the first, keeping the spacing between the strings even. Though I'm placing these at ⅜" (10mm), you can always adjust the spacing and decide what suits your playing style best.

Add the other two strings.

**30A**

Add a string tree to the longest string.

**30B**

And another string tree to the next longest string, if necessary. Tune your guitar and jam!

**30** **Add string trees.** Tension the strings, but before final tuning, we need to add a couple of screws to serve as string trees. These screws help to fine-position the strings side-to-side, but they'll also provide a little downward pressure, which increases the string "break"–the angle at which the string leaves the nut. A bigger break angle makes for a crisper sound and reduces the incidence of string buzz. The farthest posts from the nut always have the least string break, so I'm giving those two some help.

**31** **Tune the guitar.** Time to tune it up and take it for a test drive! Three-string cigar box guitars can be played in a number of different tunings. For starters, I'm going to suggest you tune your guitar so your strings sound E—B—E. This is an "open" tuning, which means the guitar plays an E chord when you strum it without fretting any strings. It will also sound a different chord when you hold the slide against the strings at any point along the neck. Open tuning is one of the keys to slide playing.

# GALLERY: BASIC CBGS

Here's a taste of a few more CBGs on the rustic side, just to show that you can make an instrument that sounds good and looks good without going overboard on setting frets and installing electronics.

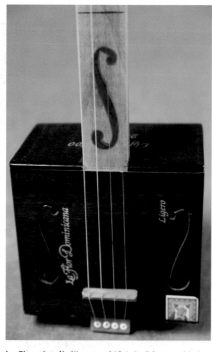

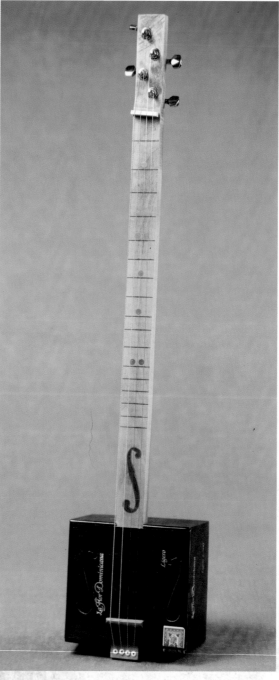

**La Flor.** Four-string fretless guitar. The builder has used red marker to indicate fret lines and decorate the fretboard.

**La Flor, detail.** Nice use of "S-holes" for sound holes.

**La Flor, bridge.** This bridge looks like it might be Corian, a material that can be worked with woodworking tools but has a nice density for transferring sound.

INSTRUMENTS OWNED BY WILLIAM J. JEHLE.



CIGAR BOX GUITARS

**Fonseca, one-string guitar.**
A nicely built one-string guitar made from a broom handle and a cigar box.

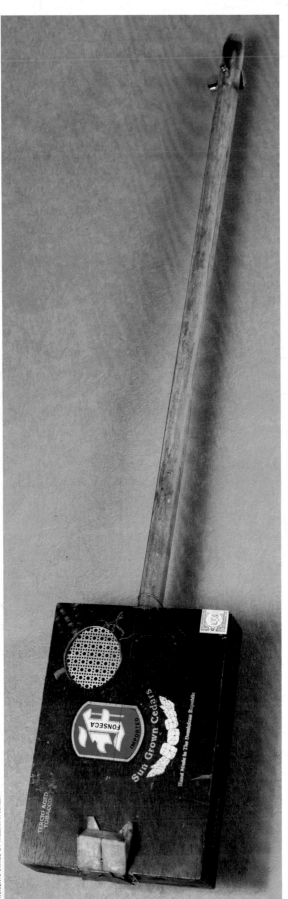

**Fonseca, headstock.** The guitar tuner used on this one-string is held in place with a bent nail.

**Fonseca, tailpiece.** The bent scrap-metal that serves as a bridge and saddle gives this guitar a very bright, powerful, and clear tone.

**Tin cigar box, bridge.** Integrated string-anchor and bridge.

**Tin cigar box, headstock.** Three-on-a-plate tuners installed with tuners forward.

**Tin cigar box three-string guitar.** This build, by Al Hamilton of State College, PA, is part of Shane Speal's collection.

**York Imperials, three-string guitar.** This build, by Al Hamilton of State College, PA, is part of Shane Speal's collection.

**York Imperials, headstock.** Three-on-a-plate tuners installed with tuners forward.

**York Imperials, detail.** This guitar has Indian head pennies embedded in the neck and tailstock.

# MATT CRUNK
## DECATUR, ALABAMA

*Tattoo artist/guitarist/singer/songwriter/guitar collector Matt Crunk attended a KISS concert when he was 11, then begged his parents for a guitar for a solid month until they finally yielded, bringing him a Gibson Les Paul on his 12th birthday. We met at his shop, Ink City Tattoo in Decatur, Alabama, the weekend of the Cigar Box Guitar Extravaganza in nearby Huntsville.*

On a visit to Memphis in 2001, Matt Crunk saw John Lowe playing his Lowebow out on Beale Street and stopped to listen for a while. "I thought it was fascinating that a modern musician was playing a cigar box guitar on the street."

Matt had played guitar in bands since he was a teenager. His heyday was as lead guitarist and singer for Fifi and the MudCats, a blues show band that toured the southeast through most of the nineties. Crunk has seen a lot of guitars—he collects them—but he'd never seen anything like the thing John Lowe was thrashing there on Beale Street.

Seeing Lowe on the street stirred up a memory, too. In the mid-nineties, Crunk had spent time with bluesman Johnny Jenkins, an old timer who had been associated with the Allman Brothers in the late sixties … before they were the Allman Brothers.

"I got to chauffer him (he didn't have a driver's license) from Nashville back to his home in Macon, Georgia." On the trip, Jenkins told Matt stories about learning to play on guitars made from discarded cigar boxes.

"I remember him telling me how he built his first guitar, taking a cigar box and a broom and a piece of wire from a screen door 'cause he couldn't afford a guitar. I'd heard about other artists who started out playing cigar box guitars."

"I wanted to build one of my own."

Matt researched John Lowe and on his next trip to Memphis, he stopped in for a visit at Lowe's store, Xanadu Books and Music. "I played one of his guitars and talked to him a little bit." In March of 2005, Crunk began research for his cigar box guitar

project. His search led him to the Yahoo forum, CIGARBOXGUITARS, where he quickly became an active participant. "Eventually I built my own version of the Lowebow—I tried not to copy him exactly, but I liked the concept of the double dowel neck, so that's what I used."

Some friends had recently opened Flying Monkey Arts, a new venue in an old factory in Huntsville. Drawing on his touring experience, Crunk helped out by booking shows for them. Seeing the level of interest and enthusiasm in the Yahoo group, Matt figured he could probably put a Cigar Box Guitar festival together. He put the word out on the forum and soon enough, cigar box guitar enthusiasts from across the country were volunteering to participate without any guarantees.

The first ever Cigar Box Guitar Extravaganza took place at Flying Monkey Arts in June of 2005. Among the performers at the first Extravaganza? None other than John Lowe. ∎

**Matt Crunk.** Crunk started the Cigar Box Guitar Extravaganza in Huntsville, Alabama after seeing John Lowe performing on the street in Memphis.

# DIANE SUTLIFF
## CHICAGO, ILLINOIS

*I spoke with Diane Sutliff at her home on Chicago's north side. Her house is littered with musical instruments, both of her own making and commercially built. A bookcase filled with empty cigar boxes hints at things to come.*

Diane Sutliff builds and plays cigar box guitars and dulcimers. Her instruments are artistic, inventive, easy to play, and beautiful. She styles the instruments she builds to be user friendly, because Diane wants *everyone* to experience the joy of making music. With her infectious enthusiasm, she has become an ambassador and has even organized and taught cigar box guitar workshops.

Sutliff recognizes that not all obstacles to musicality are mechanical. "Particularly in an urban area, like Chicago, where there are so many talented musicians performing every single night, it's hard to get people to pick up an instrument and give it a try. They don't want to make 'bad' music." Though she has installed pickups in some of her instruments, she primarily builds acoustics in order to encourage potential musicians. "Music should be a friendly, social event. Once you plug in, it's not friendly anymore; it's a performance."

Diane's speedy verbal style and natural enthusiasm help her keep the attention of the elementary school kids she works with as an itinerant art teacher with the Chicago public school system. Her orientation as a teacher may be part of what led her to develop a particularly user-friendly instrument; one a child can pick up and start playing in a matter of minutes.

Diane describes herself as a "mid-life-crisis musician." With a guitarist husband and her three growing children all showing some musical aptitude, she found she wanted to play along. She had tried to play her husband's guitars, but found them too big. "I have the hands of a child," she says, and making the chord shapes seemed torturous to her.

Diane set her sights on the fiddle due to its slender neck and manageable number of strings. In 2005, she started taking classes at Chicago's legendary Old Town School of Folk Music. Before too long, she was attending weekly fiddle jams. After a couple of years, Diane found herself drawn to another instrument that fit her hands and her style—the mandolin—and undertook learning to play that.

After spotting a unique but expensive instrument at an art fair that "looked like a canoe paddle," Diane purchased a similar instrument on eBay and began experimenting. The instrument's narrow neck was easy for her to get her hands around, and the diatonic fret scale* made it simple to pick out tunes. True, the instrument's neck was a bit long and narrow, and its slender body a bit ungainly, but Diane still enjoyed playing it. The instrument's simplicity encouraged experimentation and improvisation.

One day, while searching YouTube for tutorials relating to her new "imperfect but fun instrument," Diane saw a picture of a cigar box guitar. "I just stopped. It was like a bad zoom from a sixties movie—ziip!—I said, 'All right, I'm building one.'"

Sutliff built her first cigar box guitar from a kit. The plans called for a 24" scale length—too long for a woman oriented to fiddles and mandolins. She immediately customized the plans, using a more comfortable 17" scale. The minute she completed her kit, Diane had the bug, and she quickly discovered a truth she has watched others discover many times—"Nobody builds just one of these." As of this writing, she had built over seventy cigar box-based instruments.

**Diane Sutliff.** Diane Sutliff and one of her twin-cigar-box mountain dulcimers.

\* A diatonic scale is musical scale comprising only the whole steps in any given key. It leaves out the half-steps or sharps and flats, like a standard harmonica.

Diane has a real affection for cigar boxes. "Look at this," she says, holding a small wooden box up to the light. "It's a perfect resonating box. What could be simpler?" Although extremely sensitive to smoke, Diane haunts cigar stores, looking for just the right box, sometimes searching for that elusive matched pair she could join together to build a cigar box mountain dulcimer. Diane has some suggestions for procuring boxes. "If you're a smoke-sensitive person hunting cigar boxes in cigar stores [many of which have smoking lounges]—avoid peak smoking times." The best time to hunt for boxes, according to Diane, is "weekdays in the summer, right after the store opens." The worst time? "Saturday afternoons in the dead of winter—I get dizzy being in there even for five minutes."

Sutliff's instruments continued to evolve in a number of ways, their design dictated in part by the tools and skills Diane has had available at any given time. Asked about her woodworking background, Diane replied "Zero." She made her first guitars using little more than a hammer, drill, screwdriver, glue, and some clamps.

She's experimented with scale length, moving from an 18" scale to a 15" scale and back, eventually settling on 17" as her preferred scale length. She likes to keep the width of the neck at an inch and a quarter. "A lot of guys like an inch and a half, but they're these big palooka guys—I'm just a little thing." She keeps the string spacing to that of a standard guitar, roughly ⅜".

Diane's interest in woodworking tends toward the pragmatic. After her first experience hand-carving a nut out of rosewood, Diane had had enough of carving: "That's a nuisance. What a pain in the neck." She quickly settled on a simpler solution, using a heavier piece of fret wire to set a "zero fret" into the neck in place of a nut. "I say just do the zero fret and be done with it. Let's be honest, people, it's a box and a stick! Get your priorities straight!"

For Diane, CBG building has been an enjoyable, ongoing process of experimentation and refinement. For example, her kit guitar used scraps of guitar purfling (decorative, stacked veneer often used around sound holes and the curved sides of guitars) for frets. For her second guitar (this one from scratch), Diane used toothpicks for frets instead. "You have to use the round toothpicks because they're hardwood. The flat ones are too soft." Toothpicks soon gave way to brass cotter pins cut to length and dressed with a file. "I made a shallow trench with a saw

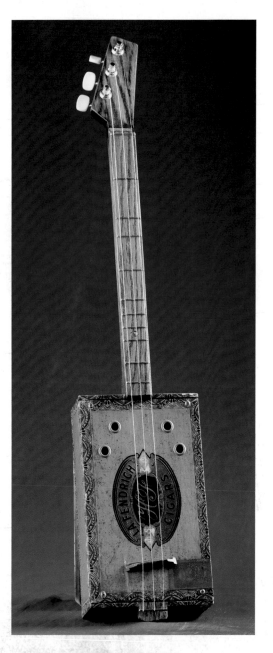

**La Fendrich.** Three-string acoustic guitar by Diane Sutliff. Sutliff often uses diatonic fretting on her instruments.

and super-glued the pins in place." The cotter pin frets played well, but they tended to pop out from time to time. Eventually, she bought a fretting saw and guide, trained herself to make fretted fingerboards, and started using conventional luthier's fret wire.

Next Diane started experimenting with variations in fretting. "Initially I was making guitars with all the frets but then I hit on this dulcimer thing [using a diatonic scale rather than a chromatic] which I think is really fascinating. That then led me into a whole education about modes and what they are, and Mixalidian and Ionian and Dorian. The dulcimer is perfectly made to explain all those concepts—so suddenly I have this understanding of things I never thought I would get."

Most importantly for Diane, using the diatonic fretting arrangement makes her instruments, and therefore the creation of music, more accessible to more people. Her inate curiosity has led her to develop a unique cigar box instrument that's neither guitar nor dulcimer. She shortened the scale so the slender neck is more manageable. She omitted a number of frets "so there are no wrong notes." She's got it tuned so that you can play a lot of music with just one or two fingers, and she's even simplified the tuning process:

Dispensing with the fretboard's conventional location dots, Diane instead employs "tuning marks." To tune the guitar, simply fret the bottom string at the dot and tune the middle string to that pitch. Repeat the process with the middle string to tune the top string. Diane makes dots by taking a paper punch to fancy pearlescent guitar picks and setting them into shallow holes made with a Forstner bit.

Though her distinctive instruments have proven popular, Diane's not interested in doing production runs. She recently built a dozen similar instruments for a workshop she conducted and that cured her of any desire to

**Diane Sutliff's cookie tin guitars.** Sutliff transferred her cigar box guitar building skills to make guitars out of cookie tins. Note the painted headstocks, diatonic frettng, and tuning dots.

become a manufacturer. Instead, she's turning her attention to new interests and challenges. Both driven and inventive, Diane finds herself "in pursuit of perfection now. I want to make each one a little better."

She's found, for example, that she can take two identical cigar boxes and bind them together to make sweet sounding mountain dulcimers. At this writing, she's building her first cigar box kalimba (an African finger piano) and is thinking about building a stand-up bass. "It's like swinging through the jungle. Ooo! A new vine! And now I'm going off into the kalimba thing—though I do have to make a few of more mountain dulcimers…" and Diane Sutliff is off and running, offering an enthusiastic, rapid-fire run-down of the next six or seven instruments she plans to build—cigar box guitars perhaps just a stop along the way. ■

# BILL JEHLE:
## DETRITOMUSICOLOGIST
### DECATUR, ALABAMA

*I had the pleasure of interviewing Bill Jehle at The Nook, a warm, friendly tavern on Bob Wallace Avenue in Huntsville, Alabama. We met on the eve of the 2010 Cigar Box Guitar Extravaganza.*

*Jehle had brought an assortment of cigar box guitars along, all of which he'd built, and leaned them against a nearby table. Huntsville has an unusual wealth of capable guitarists. Jehle had also brought a tiny amplifier he'd made, so, during our conversation, a steady stream of young men approached, asked about the instruments, and sat down to play for a bit.*

Although cigar box guitar historian and museum curator Bill Jehle definitely takes the do-it-yourself instruments seriously, he also understands the irony of devoting so much attention to what he describes as "detritomusicology."

"What is so funny about having a cigar box guitar museum is that these really were things that were either toys, or they were trash, or they were experiments—a lot of them were not seriously made to be played at all—so it's funny to elevate that to a museum artifact where it's hanging on the wall with a little plaque and you can't touch it, can't play it, you can't listen to it—because it's in the museum," says Jehle. "The irony is that I could walk around a parking lot and pick up boxes—trash that's out there—then rearrange it, and put it together, and somebody would be willing to pay for it as a work of art. It was just trash, and I was re-purposing it and turning it into something else.

"At this point, I have a least 100 different instruments, and 100 different people that made them. A hundred different people that took bits and pieces of trash—but 'trash' isn't the right word for it; I call it 'detritus'—and they recycled it and re-purposed it."

And, to be sure, Jehle has done a fair share of his own "re-purposing."

Not only has he created cigar boxes guitars—and helped expand and develop the museum that displays historic examples of the instruments—but he has also created

instructional how-to CDs and DVDs for building them, and helped organize concerts featuring the instruments. In December 2010, Jehle published *One Man's Trash: A History of the Cigar Box Guitar*, which documents the more than 150-year history of the cigar box guitar, its origins, and its changes in value and perception from the mid-1800s to the present.

The path Jehle has followed while undertaking these initiatives and pursuing his interest in CBGs illustrates the inventiveness and

ingenuity that are an integral part of the ethos and attraction of the DIY instruments.

Jehle's interest in guitars dates back to his youth. "I got interested in playing the guitar from seeing Roy Clark on TV," says Jehle, "and, when I was 10 or 12, I actually started taking guitar lessons."

As he got older, he played in bands and wrote songs, although "making money while playing in a band just never happened," said Jehle. Jehle recorded original songs in his home studio. One frustration with those recordings, recalls Jehle,

**William Jehle.** William J. Jehle, curator of the National Cigar Box Guitar Museum.

**"Junk" guitar.** Bill Jehle built this six-string electric cigar box guitar while filming his second instructional DVD on how to build a cigar box guitar. Using only an electric drill, Jehle combined a discarded broom handle, the remnants of a plastic comb, and a 99 cent pickup to create a fully playable six-string electric guitar.

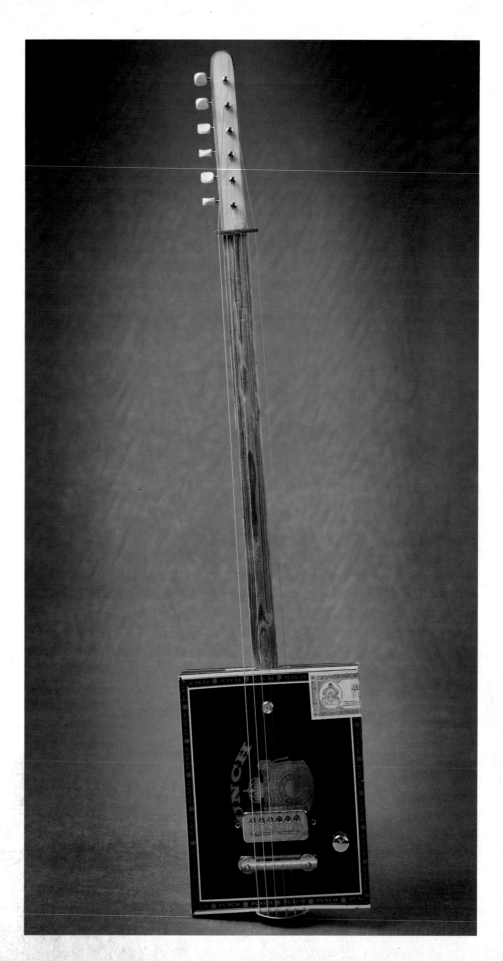

was that "there was lots of background noise and hiss and hum. I figured that a lot of noises were coming from the guitars, so I decided to build my own guitar for recording, and I wanted to make sure that it would be a perfectly quiet guitar."

As is his habit, he searched the Web extensively to learn more about guitar-making, and "I got hooked up to all these serious guitar-building sites—I was (member) number 37 on the Project Guitar Web site," says Jehle.

Then a key turning point came in 2006, when *Make Magazine* published a how-to article about cigar box guitars. "My friend from up in Detroit sent me an e-mail about the *Make* article," recalls Jehle. "I saw the article, and I freaked out." Jehle was instantly enchanted by the elegant simplicity of cigar box guitars.

As he learned about building CBGs and began to put together some of his own, "I started putting up pictures—and basically photo blogs—of building the guitars, and people started getting interested in how I made them. Eventually, I came up with an enhanced CD you could play in a computer. Half of the CD was a bunch of original tunes, and the other half was video about how I built the guitars on which I was playing the songs."

Jehle soon learned another lesson about re-purposing. "When the CD first came out, it completely flopped because I was trying to sell it as an audio CD with bonus guitar-building information, and nobody bought it. After about 6 months, I flipped it and repackaged it, basically saying, 'Here's a CD about building a guitar, with some bonus audio tracks'—and it took off like mad."

Jehle's interest quickly went beyond just making cigar box guitars, and he began to collect instruments that had been built by others. "I had cigar box violins, ukuleles, banjos, guitars and … (even) a handful of cigar box mandolins," says Jehle.

He also began to develop an interest in the history of these do-it-yourself instruments.

"I kept finding articles and magazines," says Jehle. "I wound up subscribing to newspaper archives and started getting these little things like one-line mentions 'so-and-so played a cigar box guitar on the boat dock last night' and things like that."

One interesting thing he learned was that, "It just so happened that the cigar box itself came out as an invention around the 1840s, which is ironically about the same time that we have the first written evidence of the cigar box violin," says Jehle.

Prior to that, cigars were loosely packaged in bundles and shipped in large barrels. "Before that," says Jehle, "people used packing crates, biscuit tins, hat boxes—anything that was laying around" to build stringed instruments. It appears that, when the cigar box came on the scene, it almost immediately became the detritus of choice for homemade instruments.

Jehle also found documentation of extensive use of CBGs in vaudeville. "I remember thinking that vaudeville was about the lowest level I could go and still find evidence of these things being played," says Jehle. "The people that get associated with playing a cigar box instrument are typically poor or don't have the means to get a real instrument. As soon as they did get instruments that were real or traditional, they would discard the cigar box version and never play it again. So in countless books and biographies … 'so and so got started on cigar box guitars'… the rest of the book they never bring it up again."

Jehle also began to see connections between the history of cigar box guitars and other historical developments, including the evolution of paper production and publishing, the industrialization and production of commodity goods, and interest in waste reuse and recycling. "By the mid-20th century, the cigar box guitar as a legitimate instrument waned. It wouldn't become popular again until the late-20th century, when the Internet connected like-minded guitar makers and players to seek out new sounds—something lost by our pursuit of the perfect guitar, just intonation, and meticulous setup. A cigar box guitar releases both makers and players alike to enjoy them for their quirks and imperfections."

The growing cigar box boom also got a big boost from the same *Make* magazine article that riveted Jehle's attention. "Interest exploded after O'Reilly published the "How to build a cigar box guitar" article. From that point, it started spreading like wildfire; people were making these things everywhere. Everybody got on the Internet and started posting their own variations," recalls Jehle. "That's what got me kick-started. It wasn't that I hadn't heard of it; it's just that I hadn't considered them. *Make* started a snowball rolling downhill."

As his collection of instruments, information, and historical insights grew, "I began to develop the idea of collecting all this stuff into a history," says Jehle. "I couldn't find it all in one spot."

Jehle's continuing research also led him to Shane Speal. "When you start searching about cigar box guitars, the first name you come across is Shane Speal, over and over again," says Jehle. "He's done really well to put his name out there—it has become basically synonymous with 'cigar box guitar'—and he had a cigar box guitar museum, including a whole bunch of these things that date back to the 1800s. He was able to market himself so effectively that people would eventually seek him out and say, 'Hey, I heard you have the museum … here's something that my grandfather made,'" says Jehle. "It just came from everywhere."

When Speal decided to sell his museum, his first step was to offer it to Jehle. "He sent me an e-mail—'I'm going to sell the museum—lock, stock, and barrel—and you're the first guy who comes to mind,'" recalls Jehle. "I jumped at it. He quoted a price, I said 'yes'; then I started making payments, and he started boxing up the cigar box guitars and sending them over."

Since the acquisition, Jehle has been expanding the museum collection. "People have been offering me things, and I do a lot of stuff on trade," says Jehle. "Eventually, I had an entire room just covered up to the ceiling and hanging from the walls with examples that spread from 1884 up to the present day."

After publishing his history book in December 2010, Jehle turned his interest to other projects, including a set of guitar-related videos that would be sequels to those he currently offers. Jehle's pet project is to build the ultimate made-from-scratch guitar, including the construction of a tube amp made from discarded and reused radio parts. Jehle has described this project as a way of achieving his mission "to build an entire guitar made for free."

More generally, Jehle describes his experience with cigar box guitars as having "completely changed the way I thought about guitars—completely." As Jehle has noted on his website, "There's so much more to cigar box guitars than I ever imagined. It's amazing that a $25 guitar changed the way that I look at the world." ∎

**Recycled comb.** String nut carved from a comb Jehle found at a gas station.

"I have always wanted to build my own guitar. . . .As I started to research lutherie techniques, I came to the realization that without instruction I could invest quite a bit of money and time and end up with a piece of junk. I had known about cigar box guitars and decided to build a few to work out the issues of scale, intonation, setup, etc. for a lot less money than a 'standard' guitar...And now I could care less if I ever build a 'standard' guitar."

— **B. TAL, HANDMADE MUSIC CLUBHOUSE**

# HISTORIC GALLERY

Here are just a few of the instruments in Bill Jehle's collection. Cigar boxes have been used to make instruments ever since they were first created.

**Child's six-string, detail of headstock.** Note the hand-carved tuners.

**Child's six-string, detail of bridge/saddle.** The strings were secured by pushing dowels into the holes in the bridge.

**Child's six-string CBG.** Tiny cigar box guitar ca. 1920. The builder cut a cigar box in half and made a miniature six-string instrument for a child. It has hand-carved tuners and a very small neck.

**Long-necked fretless ukulele, headstock.** Close-up of hand-carved pine tuning pegs.

**Long-necked fretless ukulele, bridge.** Ingenious use of wooden dowels to create the saddle/bridge.

**Long-necked fretless ukulele.** Cross between a guitar and ukulele instrument. The four strings, with neck-through-body construction, is reminiscent of a banjo.

**Uncle Enos banjo, headstock.** The painted headstock has been decorated with a cut-out picture of a rose.

**Uncle Enos banjo, tuning peg.** Close-up showing the violin tuning peg.

**Uncle Enos banjo, string anchor.** The wire strings for the Uncle Enos are anchored by wrapping them around the heads of protruding nails.

**Uncle Enos banjo.** This is Jehle's best example of an "Uncle Enos" banjo, built ca. 1910.

**Owl cigar box fiddle and bow.**
This fiddle, made from an "Owl Brand" cigar box, has an owl's head carved into the headstock. The bow is also handmade. The builder and vintage are both unknown.

INSTRUMENTS OWNED BY WILLIAM J. JEHLE.

**Owl cigar box fiddle, string anchor.** The builder used a piece of bone tied on with cord to anchor the strings.

**Owl cigar box fiddle, headstock.** A detail of the owl carved into the headstock.

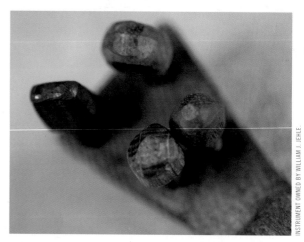

**Inside out ukulele, tuners.** Close-up of tuners. One appears to be a replacement.

**Inside out ukulele, headstock.** Headstock showing carved nut and hand-carved tuners.

**"Inside out" cigar box ukelele, ca 1920.** This tiny ukulele was built from the wood of a discarded cigar box. It's called "inside out" because the box's label is visible on the inside of the ukulele. Though it's more a piece of folk art than a playable instrument, the one remaining string is gut.

**Inside out ukulele, bridge.** Carved bridge showing gut string.

# ERIC BAKER

## COLUMBUS, OHIO

I talked to Eric Baker at the York, PA, CBG festival in 2010. I'd heard him perform, both with his band, Seven Hill Stomp, and with Shane Speal the night before the festival.

Baker is an Ohio native, a master electrician, and the founder/producer of the first cigar box guitar oriented podcast, Joker's Cigar Box Guitar Podcast.

**Seven Hill Stomp.** Baker's band, Seven Hill Stomp, played at the York, PA, CBG festival in 2010.

Eric Baker started playing guitar around the age of 14, like a lot of guys. He'd been given a Les Paul by a particularly generous uncle, and made his way through various musical phases—notably metal and punk. Prior to that, he'd played trumpet in the grade school, and then baritone in high school, but eventually set aside playing music in favor of listening to it. His tastes ran from reggae to U2, from Pink Floyd to the John Spencer Blues Explosion.

Baker was just starting to develop a taste for roots and Delta blues when, in 2007, he found himself on a job with another electrician who was a harmonica player. "He said he was a blues harp player and had won a competition in Carrollton, Kentucky. I live kind of close to Carrollton in Cincinnati, so I did an Internet search for blues festivals in Carrollton. What actually came up first was the page for the original cigar box guitar fest in 2004." Kurt Schoen [turbodiddley.com] had hosted that festival, which featured Shane Speal and Gerry Thompson, among others.

"Like a lot of people, I had never heard of a cigar box guitar." Baker waded tentatively in to the world of cigar box guitars, initially following the movement at a distance. He read about the Huntsville Extravaganza in 2007 and watched Max Shores' documentary, *Songs Inside the Box*. Occasionally, he'd find videos people had posted to YouTube, and he began following the Yahoo forum.

"One day, I decided I could probably build one of those. I got the stick; I got the box; I put some strings on it. It's one of the ones I still play, that first CBG I built. My first expectation was that it wasn't going to sound like anything, and I was pleasantly surprised when it did make a sound."

"If you're a builder, a player, or just a member, Cigar Box Nation is like a brotherhood—everybody is willing to help you succeed. . . . Personally I consider [CBG building] to be an art form and, at the same time, a form of self-expression. The thing I like most is that there's no right or wrong way to play it or build it. . . .I've always had an interest in making my own guitar. Now, thanks to Cigar Box Nation and its members, I can scratch one off the bucket list."

**—TOM CANESCHI, CIGAR BOX NATION**

Under the company name Joker Cigar Box Guitars, Baker built and sold dozens of instruments to buyers in Australia, New Zealand, Spain, and the UK. He soon realized, though, that performing was closer to his heart. "I just didn't have it in me to make a business out of building."

"I really started building CBGs to play. I started playing slide on them, and watching what some of the other guys were doing, trying to learn some of those blues rhythms. To me that's what really fits on the cigar box guitar—those blues rhythms, the blues scale. It started me wanting to play music again; wanting to play guitar again."

The desire to play took root for Baker when he attended the Cigar Box Guitar Extravaganza in Huntsville in 2008. There, he met David Williams (aka One String Willie). "He said 'You know, your guitars look nice and building's a lot of fun, but you really need to start playing.' I took it to heart and started playing. I kept playing and started writing my own songs. I was able to bring in my punk background and meld it with blues. I'm into gospel music, too, and I can do all three and nobody bats an eye. The people who are into cigar box guitars really accept [the music] for what it is." Now, Baker has performed at several open mics in the Cincinnati area. He's performed twice at the Huntsville Extravaganza, and in August 2010, he added the York, PA festival to his CV.

The cigar box guitar helped to rekindle Baker's love of music. "I was at a point with music where I wasn't inspired by what I was hearing on the radio. I desired more out of music. What this instrument did was open up a whole new world of music that didn't really have any rules, not just with how you build 'em, but the music you play on them. I always had trouble with frets and with a six-string guitar anyway. Music just seems to flow from a three-string, fretless instrument.

"I do a lot of recording, just working on my songs and working on my stage presence and my set list and making it something original and unique".

Baker enjoyed playing and recording so much that he started a podcast featuring other musicians playing cigar box guitars. "The Joker's Cigar Box Guitar Podcast recently moved over to *cigarboxguitar.com*. I do it all for free; I promote these guys, and if they want to get a CD out there, I put it out there for them."

He produces his podcast in a radio show format, usually with a theme. "I did one show just on John Henry. Everybody submitted songs—their own take on the ballad of John Henry—and I did some history of John Henry. I did one show that was all gospel, and did some history of Blind Willie Johnson and gospel blues, and played all gospel tunes. Sometimes a show just promotes a genre—I did a whole show on punk and blues. I did a whole show on Shane Speal; one on Right-On John."

Like a lot of other guys, Eric Baker has found inspiration, expression, community— even some healing—through music he creates on a crude, handmade guitar he built with his own hands. "The biggest surprise for me is that I'm able to perform in front of people. I was an introverted kid. I used to be terrified—even when I performed in band as a kid, playing a solo terrified me." With his cigar box guitar in hand, though, the terror subsides. "I feel very comfortable up there. I surprised myself with that. That wasn't expected." ■

# Build #2:
# FRETTED THREE-STRING WITH PIEZO PICKUP

Our second build, while similar to the first, will introduce a number of refinements to the cigar box guitar. We'll reinforce the neck for added stability; we'll add a fretboard and frets so you can set your slide aside, if you wish, and begin playing individual notes and chords; and finally, we'll add ultra-simple electronics so you can play your guitar through an amplifier. Each of these refinements can be added à la carte to your future guitar builds.

As I mentioned in Build #1, string tension may eventually cause the ¾" (19mm) poplar neck to bow slightly in the direction of the strings, thereby raising the strings farther from the fretboard. Minor bowing doesn't present much of a problem for the fretless guitar, but it's a major issue with a fretted instrument. This cigar box guitar will have frets, so we'll want to stabilize the board that makes the neck, and we'll do this two different ways:

1. The addition of a second piece of wood for a fretboard will lend some stability. First, it will make the neck that much thicker. In addition, laminating two pieces of wood together sets up opposing grain patterns, which reduces the tendency of the wood to warp.

2. Inside the guitar, I'll be adding a second piece of ¾" (19mm) lumber to the back of the first. This helps out in several ways. Since we'll be cutting away part of the neck that's hidden inside the guitar (to allow the "soundboard" to vibrate more freely and to make room for the pickup), that board will need the extra support. It'll also provide just a bit more mass, which will improve sustain—the ability of the strings to continue vibrating when they're plucked or struck.

This build provides you with an opportunity to overcome your fear of fretting, like I did, and provides detailed instructions for installing frets in a cigar box guitar.

For those who wish to go electric, I'll also provide instructions for installing a simple, inexpensive piezo pickup, volume control, and associated wiring.

Each of these refinements can be added to your cigar box guitar projects individually or together. My intention here is to provide you with options for customizing your own cigar box guitar projects. When it comes to customizing options, these three are really just the tip of the iceberg!

## MATERIALS

- Wooden cigar box
- Half a set of classical guitar tuners (tuners for a slotted headstock), or three single tuners
- ³⁄₁₆" (5mm) brass machine screw with two nuts
- Moderately hard material for a nut (hardwood, rosewood, buffalo horn, Corian, or other)
- 36" (915mm)-long 1x2 (19 x 38mm), hardwood (avoid pine, cedar, poplar, or other soft woods)
- 18" (460mm)-long 1x2 (19 x 38mm), hardwood (avoid pine, cedar, poplar, or other soft woods)
- ⅛" x 2" (3 x 50mm) bird's eye maple or similar, 30" (760mm) long for a fretboard
- ⅛" x 3" (3 x 75mm) balsa wood, about 12" (305mm) long
- 1¼" (30mm) brass screws with decorative washers, four
- (3) Guitar strings, E—A—D or G—B—E
- Piezo buzzer
- ¼" (6mm) mono phone jack
- Light insulated wire in two colors

## TOOLS AND SUPPLIES

**NECESSARY:**

- Four-in-hand rasp/file combo
- Wood glue
- Thick super glue
- Square
- Pencil or marking knife
- Yardstick or tape measure
- Masking tape or painter's tape
- Several clamps
- Small handsaw
- Phillip's head screwdriver
- Hand drill, powered or otherwise
- Drill bits
- ¼" (6mm) Forstner bit
- Sheet of plain paper
- Utility knife
- Tung oil, shellac, or finish of choice
- Torch tip cleaners
- Pliers
- Soldering iron and solder
- Volume knob or stock to make one
- Guitar pick
- Paper punch

**FOR INSTALLING FRETS:**

- Fret saw or other fine-kerf saw
- Rawhide mallet
- Flush nippers
- Fret beveling file

**HELPFUL:**

- Handplane
- Marking (scratch) awl
- Marking knife
- Drill press
- Sharp shop knife
- Amplifier (borrowed if you don't own one)
- 2" (50mm) chisel and mallet
- Rasps and files, flat, curved, and round
- Small parts vise or equivalent
- Curved spokeshave

**Parts and pieces.** Moving clockwise from the wooden cigar box: brass machine screw with two matching nuts; rosewood off-cut pieces to support the nut; 3' (915mm) of maple fretboard; two pieces of roughly 1x2 (19 x 38mm) cabinet project scraps; half a set of used classical (slotted headstock) guitar tuners; a piezo buzzer; and a ¼" (6mm) mono phone plug jack with shielded wire already soldered in place.

**Defining the headstock.** Line up the tuners against the long piece of lumber to determine the length of the headstock. Place a pencil mark at the nut line.

**Removing the finish from cabinet scraps.** I start by using a smoothing plane to take the finish off the lumber I found. You may prefer sanding; planing produces less dust. On the other hand, your wood may not have a finish that needs removing as mine did.

**Locating the bridge.** I settled on a 24" (610mm) scale, and, inspired by my Gibson Firebird, I moved the bridge a little farther up the box so the guitar ends up with a nice, long neck. Measure from the nut line down 24½" (622mm) and place another mark on the neck board to locate the bridge. Lay the neck board on top of the box so the bridge mark lines up between ⅓ to ½ of the distance from the tail end. Place a piece of tape on the box to mark the location.

**Marking the portion of the neck that will be inside the box.** Using a large clamp to hold the two pieces together, mark the neck with a marking knife to indicate the outside edges of the box sides.

**Transferring the line.** Using a marking knife makes it exceptionally easy to transfer lines to adjacent sides. Rather than trying to line up the square by eye, just place the marking knife into the groove you've already made and slide the square up to the knife.

**Cutting the support board to length.** Line up the support board next to the box wall indicators on the neck. Cut the support board so it fits flush with the bottom end of the box and extends 1½" (38mm) beyond the top end of the box.

**Cut the angle in the support board.** Flip the support board on its side and cut a 45° slice from the end.

**Round and smooth the top of the support board.** Use a four-in-hand on the end of the support board to round and smooth the part that will protrude from the box. It's cosmetic, yes, but it's also for comfort, if you happen to be playing the high notes way up the neck. Looks good!

**Rounding the tailstock.** Now, use the four-in-hand to round the end of the neck board where it will protrude from the bottom of the box.

**Clamp the boards together.** The next step is to clamp the two pieces together. Set the assembly aside to allow ample drying time. Keep the clamps on for at least 30 minutes, but don't do any work to the boards or stress them in any way for 24 hours.

**Glue the support board to the neck board.** Carefully line up reference marks and spread glue on the two surfaces.

**Cut the fretboard to length.** After squaring the top edge of the fretboard (the thin piece of wood the frets will be set into), line that end up with the nut line you drew on the neck assembly. The string nut will nest against the end of this fretboard in the "zero" fret position. Then, cut this fretboard to length—that is, cut it off where it meets the cigar box lid so it butts up against the lid without going under it.

**Glue and clamp.** Glue the fretboard in place. Clamp and let the assembly dry for 24 hours.

**True up the edge.** Go back to your hand plane (or rasp or file) to even up the edges of the three boards and remove excess glue.

**Mark the headstock for tuners.** Remove the posts from your tuners by backing out the tiny Phillips head screws that hold the posts in place. Place the metal plate flat against the headstock so you can get accurate placement on the holes the posts will seat into. Use an awl to mark placement of the tuner posts as well as the screw holes for the screws that hold the tuners in place.

**Carry the center lines around to the front.** Use your marking knife to bring a line from the tuning post center points around to the front of the headstock. This will help you locate the cutout in the headstock.

**Cut the headstock slot.** Reach for the 2" (51mm) chisel to chop, then carve, most of the remaining wood from the slot area.

**Drill out pilot holes for the headstock cutout.** We're going to open up the headstock. With this style of tuner, the guitar strings pass through the headstock to wrap around the tuners. Using a ⅝" (16mm) Forstner or a spade bit (diameter slightly smaller than you want the final cutout to be), drill holes to clear out most of the wood. In the inset photo, you can see that the holes aren't in a perfect line, but they all lie within the marks on the side (I started a little close to the nut—I think it'd be better to position the bottom of this cutout at least an inch from the nut).

**Finish the slot shape.** Finish creating the slot shape with rasps, files, and a little sandpaper.

**Back to the box.** The next step is one you're familiar with from the first guitar—notching out the box to accept the neck—but I'm going to show you a math-free method for finding center lines and locating the neck. You don't even have to choose between metric and English—you don't need a ruler. Place a piece of plain paper under the box so one edge (the edge away from the camera in this case) lines up perfectly flush with one box edge. Using the box as a straight edge, trim the paper to the same width as the cigar box.

**Fold to locate center line.** Fold the cut-to-size sheet of paper perfectly in half, carefully lining up the edges.

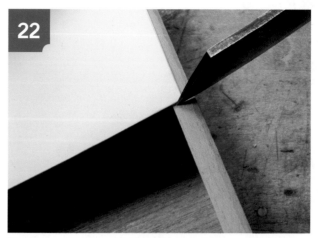

**Find the center.** Open the cigar box and align one edge of the paper gage with the edge of the cigar box. The opposite edge indicates dead center, which you should mark now with a sharp knife.

**Repeat for the neck.** Use the same method as Steps 20 and 21, using the neck as a guide, to create a neck-centering template. Fold the template carefully in half and give it a sharp crease. Open the creased paper and align the crease with the center mark on the edge of the box side you made in the previous step. Mark each side of the neck template to determine the location for the neck cutout.

**Finish marking the neck notch.** Reach for your square and, aligning it with the notches, carry a line down the side of the box.

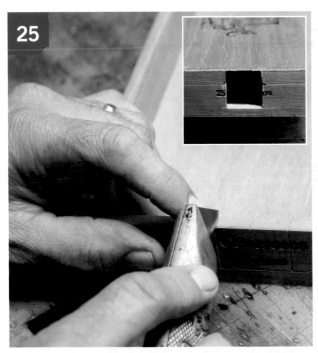

**25**

**Cut away the neck notch.** Use a utility knife to cut the sides of the box. Keep in mind that the top end of the box (pointing toward the head stock) wil have a larger cutaway than the tail end of the box because it has to accommodate the support board in addition to the neck, while the tail end just accepts the thickness of the neck. Cut the neck notch slightly smaller than you need it and file the opening to fit.

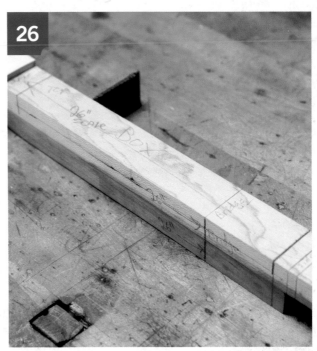

**26**

**Prepare to refine the neck thickness.** The next step will be to cut away a portion of the neck's thickness to give the soundboard freedom to vibrate in response to the strings. This will also make room for the piezo pickup, which will be sandwiched between 2 thin pieces of balsa wood. Mark the neck to leave about ½" (13mm) intact under the box top at each end for support.

**27**

**Chop out the waste.** Remove the bulk of the waste with a 2" (51mm) chisel. Use the same chisel to smooth the surface you've just chopped out. This doesn't have to be perfect, as it will be hidden anyway.

**Test fit the neck.** Put the neck into the box and close the box for a test fitting. Now it's starting to look like a guitar!

**Shape the neck.** Clamp the neck board into a vise in preparation for shaping the back of the neck to fit your hand. As with the first build, I'll use a curved spokeshave and/or a four-in-hand rasp to rough-in the contour. Here, the shape of the neck is already roughed in. Finish shaping with scrapers or files and sandpaper.

**Gather the fretting tools.** These are the essential tools for installing frets. Clockwise from left: FLAT-faced nippers, fret-cutting saw, test board, fret end file, square, and rawhide mallet. Add to the basics some sort of fret layout guide. I got an ingenious chart for just a few dollars.

## PRACTICE SETTING FRETS

First, strike a line across the board and then, using a square as a straightedge, cut a shallow slot with a fretting saw.

The side view of my test piece tells me how many saw strokes it took to reach the right depth—not many. If the slots are cut too deep, it weakens the neck and increases the likelihood of frets not seating or popping out later.

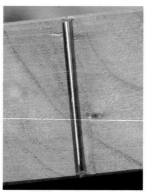

Make a shallow cut.

Slot depth.

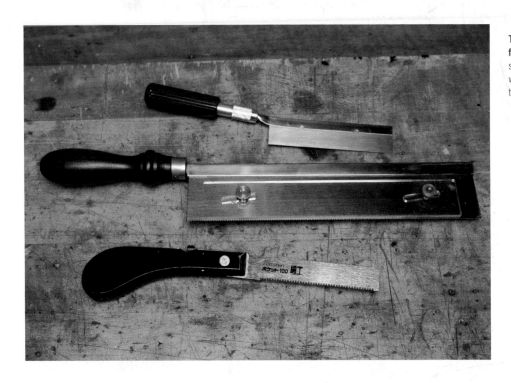

**Three saws I tested for cutting fret slots.** Top down: X-Acto Razor saw, Stewart MacDonald fretting saw with adjustable depth guide, Japanese trim saw.

## FRET CUTTING SAW

I tried all three of these saws for cutting fret slots. At top is an X-Acto Razor saw ($10). In the center is a saw with attached depth guide sold by Stewart MacDonald ($32). At the bottom is a folding Japanese trim saw ($20).

**X-Acto:** Ted Crocker suggested I try the X-Acto. The price is right. It makes a nice, narrow cut but takes a very patient, slow approach. I found the metal holding the blade to be too weak at the handle to hold the blade straight. This unsteadiness allowed for too much side-to-side flexion, making for sloppy fret slots—wider at the end than in the middle.

**StewMac:** This is probably the Cadillac of hand-fretting saws with a nice, heavy brass back to keep the blade straight and vibration free, and an attached depth guide to keep you from over-cutting. The only downsides I found: 1) The Plexiglas depth guide tended to mar the wood adjacent to the slot, and 2) Some of my more experienced woodworker friends scoffed at the depth guide.

**Japanese:** My favorite. This tiny saw has a razor sharp, micro thin blade and cuts a very narrow slot to depth in a matter of one or two pulls. Japanese saws cut on the draw or pull stroke, which has several advantages. Most notably, pulling on a piece of thin steel makes it taut, whereas pushing against the same piece of steel causes it to bow and buckle—which is why saws like the StewMac combo need a piece of heavy brass to steady them. A taut blade makes a thin, clean cut—no side-to-side flexion. The blade folds into the handle to keep it (and you) safe. One word of caution: If you forget what you're holding and try to use this like a Western saw (push/pull/push/pull), you'll bend the blade.

**Mark and saw frets.** Fold the fret chart to expose your chosen scale length (I picked 26" [660mm]) and tape the chart securely in place. Line up the square carefully with each fret line and mark each fret's location in turn. Using your saw of choice CAREFULLY saw a slot at each fret position. Too shallow and the fret won't seat properly; too deep and you weaken the wood's grip on the fret tang. I know builders who do this free-hand, and others who wouldn't think of trying it without a saw equipped with a depth gauge. Know thyself!

**Install the frets.** Work with a longer piece of fret wire and cut it off as you go. Working from one end of the fret to the other, position the tang into one end of the slot, the other end angled upward 20 or 30°, then VERY gently begin tapping the tang into place, rocking the fret quickly down into the slot as you tap along its length. Some builders prefer pressing the fret into place with a wooden caul placed in a drill press. With the fret firmly seated, clip the fret wire, leaving a small amount protruding, and move on to the next fret.

**Clip fret ends flush to the neck.** With the flat-faced fretting nippers, trim both ends of each fret flush to the neck.

**Clean up and beware the vicious ends and pieces.** These little bits can cause all kinds of problems, including, but not limited to, destroying the finish of a cigar box inadvertently placed on top of them. Cedar is SOFT. Sweep up very carefully after you've trimmed the frets flush. Remove all scraps of fret wire from work surfaces.

**35**

**File fret ends.** Using a simple, inexpensive fret end file I bought online from CB Gitty (and with a block beneath the neck for support), I file the fret ends to nice, clean, 45° angles. Keep the fret file's wood base FLAT against the fret crowns. Make sure that NONE of the tang remains protruding from the fretboard. Next, use a tiny file (an actual fret file or a spark plug file) to knock the corners off the top of each fret, making a smooth, hazard-free pathway to slide your hand up and down the neck. These fret-end files are easy to make and I know a number of builders who have made them.

**36**

**Size the post.** Find the outside diameter of the tuning post. You can measure it with a ruler or micrometer, or use a drill bit organizer or sizer (plastic drill bit sizers are available for a buck or so at hardware stores) as I have, and select the corresponding drill bit to drill placement holes in the side of the headstock where the tuners will mount.

**37**

**Drill for the tuning post.** Start with a smaller bit and drill a pilot hole for each tuning post. Move to the drill press to expand the holes and take them all the way through. This way, you can be certain the tuners will be perpendicular to the headstock, and the drill press has a depth stop so you don't go all the way through the second side.

**Test fit the tuners.** Make sure the tuners fit the holes, that they seat correctly, and that they turn freely.

**Finish the headstock.** Use something round (I used a cork stopper) as a pattern to trace a semicircle at the top of the headstock.

**Finish the neck.** Use tung oil to finish the neck. Tung oil is simple to use—wipe on, let sit, wipe off, steel wool. Repeat as many times as you like. Tung oil dries quickly, doesn't run, and provides a hard finished surface.

**Select nut material.** To make my string nut, I started with a piece of—I'm not making this up—water buffalo horn I got at a very reasonable price on eBay from Vietnam. You really don't have to use Vietnamese water buffalo horn for your nut. You can do just as well with a piece of very hard wood, like ebony or rosewood, or a scrap of some composite, such as Corian. Mark the nut for length (width of the neck at the top of the fretboard) and string placement. ⅜" (10mm), more or less, is a good starting point for string spacing. The nice thing about a three-string set-up is that you know the middle string will be in the center and you can work from there.

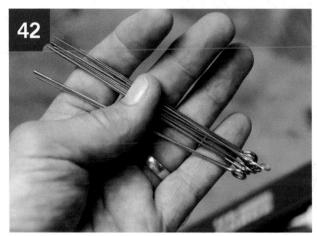

**42**

**Get out your makeshift nut files.** A set of professional nut files for varying string gauges would be nice, but they're really pricey. Ted Crocker gave me a hot tip for improvising nut files—a set of welding torch tip cleaners. Total cost, with shipping, under $10. These tip cleaners are not terribly sharp, so they cut slowly, but that's actually an advantage. As they say, it's pretty easy to cut a little more, but a real bear to back up after you've gone too far.

**43**

**File string slots.** Snug the nut into a vise—I scored this tiny example at an estate sale at the end of the last century. Rough-in the string slots in three different sizes. To determine the size of the slot, compare your torch-tip cleaners to the guitar strings you plan to use.

**44**

**Finish the string nut.** Cut the nut to length and finish the end.

**45**

**Glue the nut in place.** Use a small drop of extra-thick super glue (I recommend Gorilla Glue) to fasten the nut in place. I suggest adding a wedge of rosewood or something similar, held in place with wood glue, to support it.

**Create corner/lid supports.** Whereas the previous build was simply glued shut, I recommend leaving the innards of this guitar accessible in case you ever need to make a repair to or upgrade the electronics. In order to reinforce the corners and also to provide something to screw into when closing up the box, cut four support posts for the inside corners of the box. These need to just fit inside when the box is closed.

**Make sound holes.** I selected a three-circle pattern for the sound holes. Use masking tape to protect the box and to give a place to write on for laying out the sound holes. The tape also helps to reduce splintering. When drilling into cigar box material, ALWAYS back up the piece you're drilling into with another board to prevent tear-out, splintering, and accidentally drilling through both sides of the box! Once again, the wood used for cigar boxes is generally very, very thin and soft. If you're using a massive, heavy electric hand drill it's easy to do a lot of damage. Don't ask me how I know this.

**Find a piezo buzzer.** The piezo buzzer is available through Radio Shack, C. B. Gitty, and a number of other cigar box craft suppliers. It works on a very simple principle that I don't understand, but we're basically reversing the flow of electricity. Instead of using electricity to make a vibration (the buzzer function) we're going to turn vibrations into electricity (cigar box guitar pickup function).

**Free the piezo!** GENTLY crack open the plastic case and pry out the brass piezo element. Caution: It's very thin. If you got your buzzer from a cigar box guitar parts supplier, yours may not be housed; if so, you can skip this step.

**50**

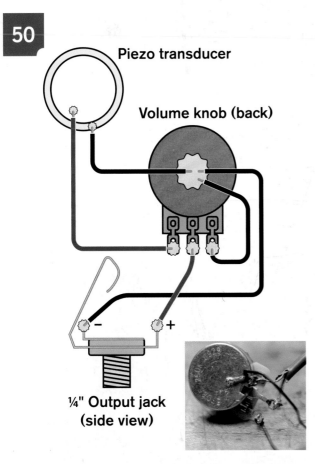

Piezo transducer

Volume knob (back)

¼" Output jack
(side view)

−  +

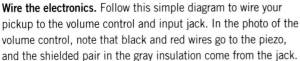

**51**

**Wire the electronics.** Follow this simple diagram to wire your pickup to the volume control and input jack. In the photo of the volume control, note that black and red wires go to the piezo, and the shielded pair in the gray insulation come from the jack.

**Make a piezo sandwich.** Compared to magnetic pickups, piezo pickups are quite vulnerable to feedback and also to transmitting and amplifying handling noises. To shield the piezo from external sounds and to dampen it a little from handling noises, secure it tightly between two pieces of balsa wood. Cut two pieces so there's room for the piezo and enough wood around it to glue the two pieces together. Glue and clamp the sandwich (inset).

**Prepare for final assembly.** Once again using painter's masking tape, lay out the bridge position and mark for pre-drilling screw holes in the corners.

**52**

**Clamp and glue the corner supports in place.** Use wood glue and clamp to attach the supports to the box. Allow the assembly to dry for 24 hours.

**Install electronics.** Drill holes in the box top to accommodate both the jack and the volume control (also called a volume pot). These are held in place by their respective retaining nuts. It's also a good idea to push a guitar cable into the jack at this point to test the fit—to make sure it goes in and stays seated.

**Take a test drive.** Before closing up the box, plug the guitar body into an amplifer to test the connections. With the amp turned on, you should be able to tap on the box and hear the taps amplified. Success!

**Add important aesthetic components (aka decorate the inside box bottom).** If I'm using sound holes that allow me to see inside my guitar, I like to dress up the box bottom a little. I've had an intuition that this guitar will just not sound right without a topographical map of the hilly Hoosier National Forest in southern Indiana—including parts of Monroe and Brown counties. Decorate your inside box bottom as you see fit.

**57**

**Add neck support blocks.** With your decorative background glued in place, cut additional blocks of wood to support the neck on either side. It's also possible to cut this whole stretch from a single block of wood. Either way works—build up or cut down. Sometimes my brain is in more of a build-up place, and sometimes more of a cut-down place.

**58**

**Close the lid.** Secure the top closed with decorative brass screws and washers. TIGHTEN GENTLY. The top, just to remind you, is really thin, and it's quite probably cedar, which is really soft. With a little too much force, these washers can turn into cookie cutters.

**59**

**Make a volume knob.** Start with a small piece of cherry and cut it to a square dimension. Locate the center and drill a pilot hole there.

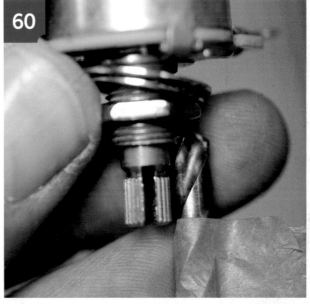

**60**

**Fit the knob to the volume pot.** Drill a hole slightly smaller in diameter than the stem of your volume pot. The stem is designed for a tension fit. Use a piece of painter's masking tape on the drill bit as a depth gauge, and drill a hole in the cherry to accept the pot's stem.

**61**

**Finish the knob.** Whittle the knob round and give it some shape, then oil-finish it and press it into place.

**62**

**Make position markers.** Diane Sutliff (page 62) showed me how to make position indicators out of flat picks. Most common paper punches punch a ¼" (6mm) hole and are strong enough to punch through a mid-weight pick. Select a pick that complements your overall theme and punch out seven or eight dots.

*"Everyone* can build a simple instrument, or play a simple tune, when there are no rules or boundaries. There is no right or wrong, just enjoyment. . . .Music should be fun and available to all—and stuff the big-name money machines! A customer of mine summed it up nicely in a recent email: 'I will be selling my Gibson Les Paul this weekend to make room for a Randy Roosters.' Proud? You betcha!"

**—ROOSTERMAN,
HANDMADE MUSIC CLUBHOUSE**

**63**

**Drill dot trenches.** Using a ¼" (6mm) Forstner bit (Forstners make a flat-bottomed hole), drill VERY SHALLOW holes (practice on a scrap) where you want position markers. I went with a common guitar arrangement of markers at positions 3, 5, 7, 9, 12 (doubled), and 15.

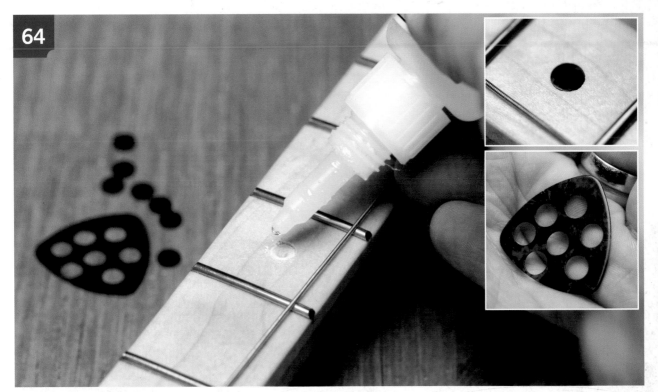

**64**

**Glue the dots in place.** Use a small quantity of extra-thick super glue to cement the dots in place. Pretty! The novelty pick is a bonus; loan it to a friend at your next gig and tell them it's a custom job.

**65**

**String it up!** This is the best part—hearing your cigar box guitar's voice for the first time. String it up and tune it. As you can see, I initially experimented with the heavier (E/A/D) guitar strings for this instrument. After hearing it, I decided this guitar was better suited for lighter strings and a higher pitch. I switched the E/A/D combo out for the G/B/E strings instead.

**66**

**Install the bridge.** The thread size of this brass screw worked well with the lighter strings. Next, I'm going to make a tail-end string tree to increase the angle of the string break and hold the strings snug against the bridge. As you can see, I've drilled two holes near the bridge.

**67**

**Make the string tree.** Clamp a ¼" (6mm) oak dowel to your bench and flatten one side with a block plane, rasp or file. Drill two holes through the dowel so the mounting screws will pass between the guitar strings.

**68**

**Attach the string tree.** Use two long brass screws to attach the string tree near the bridge.

**69**

**Apply mild pressure with the string tree.** Cinch the string tree down just enough to snug the strings.

**70**

**Install a final touch.** Giving my instrument a final going over, I noticed the strings were beginning to bite into the edge of my box, so I cut a piece of brass rod to fit and slid it into place here.

# GALLERY: FRETTED CBGS

This gallery showcases a few great examples of CBGs with frets and various treatments thereof. Take a look and get inspired!

**"Hitone" four-string electric CBG.** Four-string electric CBG built by Rob Baker, aka "Hitone," a guitar and cigar box guitar maker Jehle met through projectguitar.com. This guitar is equipped with a whammy bar fashioned out of cabinet hardware. Clever use of screw-eyes, threaded rod, and wing nuts creates a bridge.

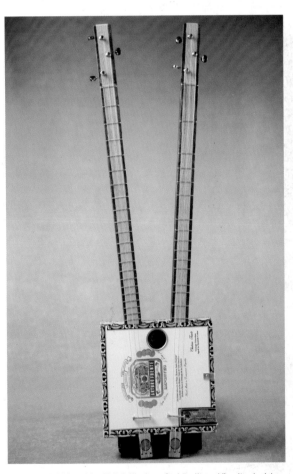

Double-neck CBG by John Nickel. Nicely crafted "split neck" guitar by John Nickel of Huntsville, Alabama. The guitar's two necks share a standard set of guitar strings with the heavier/lower strings on the upper neck and the lighter/higher strings on the bottom neck.

**"Hitone" CBG, tail.** A closer look reveals a gate hinge folded and put to work as a saddle/string anchor.

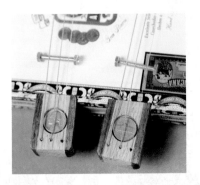

**Double-neck CBG, tailpiece detail.** Both necks are laminated from oak flanked by black walnut. Nickel "signs" his work by embedding nickles in his builds.

**Brown three-string CBG, bridge.** A bit of shape to the wooden part of the bridge creates a quiet accent.

**Brown three-string CBG.** A custom order made by Darren Brown of Nova Scotia for Shane Speal.

**Brown three-string CBG, sound holes.** The trio of graduated sound holes are simple but classy.

**Brown three-string CBG, headstock.** A bracket adds a little something to the headstock.

**Brown three-string CBG, tuners.** These "three-on-plate" tuners were cut apart and re-configured for the cigar box guitar.

**Casa Torano, tail piece detail.** A heavy brass hinge provides a solid string anchor.

**Casa Torano, three-string acoustic/piezo electric guitar.** Diane Sutliff built this three-string acoustic with a rosewood fretboard over an oak neck. She's given it chromatic (guitar) fretting.

# KEVIN M. KRAFT
## KANSAS CITY, MISSOURI

*I met with Kevin Kraft on a sunny autumn day at his home in suburban Kansas City, Missouri. When I arrived, Kevin's wife, Sharon, and their four children lined up to greet me. In a corner of the living room, a half-dozen cigar box guitars stood lined up, mirroring their owners. Hand-cut bottleneck guitar slides filled a small bookshelf attached to the wall.*

One evening, when they were eight or nine, Kevin Kraft and his twin brother Kory turned on the TV to watch *High Chaparral*. As one, the young boys decided they HAD to learn to play the show's chugging theme song on guitar. "We had some old guitars lying around the house. We didn't know how to tune them or anything like that, but we tried to mimic that sound as much as we could."

Mom Kraft soon enrolled the brothers in guitar lessons, which they continued for a short while—until it became apparent that neither Kevin nor Kory was prepared to actually *practice* their lessons. But the seed had been planted, and in very fertile ground.

The Krafts were a musical family. "My mom sang and played the xylophone. My three sisters all played in band in high school. Two of them sang pretty regularly, and one of them was an avid pianist. My oldest brother was a heck of a drummer. We had a LOT of music around the house, if we weren't playing it, we were listening to it on the record player.

"We heard so many different styles growing up. My parents loved southern gospel. My oldest sister was into everything. One of my other sisters was into the Osmond Brothers. Another liked Olivia Newton John. We also had a foster sister who listened to a lot of Motown stuff. My oldest brother loved classic rock and roll—my education in classic rock came from him."

Kevin had always been encouraged to sing. His mother had heard him singing in church and drafted him into singing in the church choir. Kraft soaked up music like a sponge. "I had an uncanny ability to mimic whatever I heard. I could do John Denver. If you hear me sing you can still hear some influences from back then. I could do a great Gordon Lightfoot. Everyone I listened to, I could mimic. But I still wanted to play, so we took what little we knew about the guitar—parts of the guitar, how to tune it—I took what I learned

Kevin Kraft. Kevin Kraft in his basement workshop in Kansas City. He's playing the first CBG he made, for which he used a silverware box.

from there and I just kept learning from different things—books and watching people. We pretty much taught ourselves to play at that point."

Kevin had a good ear. He could learn to play just about anything he wanted to. "I got pretty good, good enough to play in church for people, stuff like that. I never really did the kind of stuff that I wanted to, 'cause I wanted to do contemporary things. Ours was a pretty traditional church, so I'd scare them to death sometimes, bringing in my guitar, or even … my electric guitar."

In his teens, Kevin started singing with the organization Youth For Christ (YFC) and got a

taste of touring all over New York State. Through YFC, Kevin met another young musician named Thurlow Prescott. "We started performing what was then contemporary Christian music our senior year of high school." They had sung with YFC all over New York State. Kevin and Thurlow decided to form their own group and they called themselves Glory Flight. "So, with my guitar in tow, we became troubadours, singing everywhere we could." Glory Flight grew from a duo to a trio, eventually to a full band, then back to a trio. Ultimately they settled back into the original lineup with just Kevin and Thurlow.

Encouraged by their local success, they took off on a cross-country tour in 1982, travelling, singing, and playing in churches, civic centers, and youth centers all the way to from New York to Oregon. "Looking back on it, I'm not sure how we actually did it. We made it up as we went along, pieced together an itinerary."

On their '82 tour, Kevin and Thurlow had stopped in Kansas City, where Thurlow's sister lived. Kevin thought Kansas City would make an excellent base of operations for Glory Flight. "Where we were living was pretty isolated, very conservative," and not centrally located like Kansas City. Kevin suggested they make Kansas City their base. "So that's what we did, in 1983." Shortly after moving, Thurlow got married and started a family. Ironically, the duo broke up shortly after relocating to Kansas City. Kevin did some solo work and eventually settled into occasionally playing and singing in the church he'd joined. Kraft too, eventually married and started a family of his own. He and his wife now home-school their four children.

Though a thoroughly competent rhythm player, Kevin had not been able to play guitar leads to his satisfaction. "I have stupid fingers," he explains. "I can fake it," he admits, but he believes his life-long battle with insomnia has cost him some of his fine-motor skills. "That's the first thing to go."

He had long found himself drawn to the silky, fluid sound some guitarists produced, but was mystified at how guitarists achieved it. One day, in his mid twenties, Kevin caught an episode of VH1 featuring Bonnie Raitt. On the middle finger of her left hand, Raitt wore a glass medicine bottle that she slid up and down the strings. "THAT'S IT! That's how you do it!" Kraft says he responded. "I ran out immediately and bought a slide and began the excruciating task of learning to how to play slide guitar." It's painful, he says, because "when you're off-tune you know it … you squeak and you squawk, and it's not a pleasant experience for anyone listening—but learn it I did."

Immersing himself in slide playing, initially on the acoustic guitar, later on the electric, Kraft says he got to where he could sustain a pretty good tone. Kevin had found a sound, and he wanted to make that sound his. With the slide,

Kraft's "stupid fingers" didn't get in the way. "That's why I got so into slide; I loved it, and you don't need as much dexterity." He studied ELO's Jeff Lynne and other players he looked up at the local library: Sonny Landreth, Joe Walsh of the Eagles, and, of course, Bonnie Raitt.

"I got pretty good at it."

"I always appreciated slide guitarists like Duane Allman and Joe Walsh, who brought the slide guitar out in FRONT of the music, like a lead instrument. That's what I wanted."

As a worship leader in the church he attended with his young family, Kevin began introducing more music into the services—initially acoustic, then, gradually, electric. When worshippers acclimated to their new electrified soundtrack, Kevin saw an opportunity to debut his slide playing. Though the conservative crowd initially seemed somewhat baffled, they were at the same time "suitably entertained" . . . and the younger worshippers ate it up.

Though content with his slide playing and the way it fit into his life he still felt something missing. It could be better. He'd been playing a perfectly nice Strat-style electric guitar, but, he confesses, "I had never been totally satisfied with the sound; I knew I was missing something. I loved the old Delta sound. To me, the equipment that I was playing sounded too sophisticated. I was looking for something a little less refined, a little more woodshed, but I wasn't sure how to get it."

Naturally, Kraft started modifying his guitars—replacing nuts, experimenting with strings and pickups—but nothing worked to bring forth that more primitive sound. He kept searching. One day, in 2006, frustrated after researching guitar modifications online, digging around for ways to create the sound he hungered for, he started thinking maybe he'd have to build his own guitar from scratch. Maybe he searched for "homemade guitars," he's not sure, but somehow he came across some information about cigar box guitars.

"I remembered [as a kid] trying to make guitars out of cardboard shoe boxes, stuff like that, with rubber bands for strings, but you couldn't do anything with that. Nice idea but … cigar box guitars?"

The more he searched, the more he saw references to cigar box guitars. At first, he thought of it as a novel idea—a kid's project—but eventually he hit Shane Speal's site and became intrigued. He looked at some plans, thought about it a little more, and almost flippantly thought, "'Maybe this is what I've been looking for …' but as a joke. I wasn't really serious."

Serious or not, Kevin stopped into a Kansas City knick-knack store called Mom's Old Stuff and asked about cigar boxes. They had a few, but they were tiny. Then, he spotted an old silverware box. It was big. Kevin thought, "Now THAT's what I'm talkin' about …" He bought the box for a dollar, took it home, and set to work with his downloaded plans.

"I didn't tell anybody what I was doing down there [in his basement shop]. I secretly went to work on my 'creature' over a period of about five days." Then, it was finished. Kevin added strings and tuned it up. "Everybody was upstairs. I sat on the basement couch and strummed it for the first time. I'm like … YES!

"I started playing, you know, and I had my slide, and everybody rushed downstairs. Sharon said, 'STOP IT! That's GREAT!' All four kids immediately wanted one. That was the first one that I built and it turned out really, really well. The thing played! And it was the sound I had been waiting for."

At long last, Kevin Kraft had found his *High Chaparral*. With his new silverware box guitar and his slide playing chops, he could finally produce that insistent, chugging guitar sound he'd heard on TV and wanted so badly to make with his brother as a child.

"I'm not sure what it is. I've always been attracted to the power chord, for example. The chunky, low-end, bottom string guitars, that's

**Kraft's Cohiba CBG.** Kraft draws position markers on the side of his guitar necks, which makes them easier to see when the instrument is being played.

what attracted me most, that's what I wanted to play. The higher strings were sometimes an impediment. The three-stringers appeal to me so much."

Kraft was hooked. "I thought different boxes must have different tones," and so, in quick succession, he built two more guitars. Today, he's lost count of how many guitars he's built. He has sold a few, but he appears to be driven primarily by his passionate desire to share the sound, to share the magic. Most of the guitars he's built he's given away to family and friends.

It had been over twenty-five years since Kevin had toured with Glory Flight, but he came back to the public stage in July 2010, entering the Kansas City Blues Challenge with just a cigar box guitar and his voice. Though Kraft did not win, he made it all the way to the semi-final round of the competition. The audience response told Kraft what he needed to know. "I felt right at home doing it. The winner, Jason Vivone, loved what I did and asked if I wanted to do some more singing. He put me in touch with a couple of venues." Vivone also put Kevin in touch with the producer who has made Vivone's demo disk. At this writing, Kevin Kraft is on his way to producing his own demo which, along with some cover tunes, will also include a number of Kevin's original songs.

The Kansas City Blues Society liked Kevin's passion and asked him to join the board. He accepted, and his new post puts him in a better position to realize his dream of organizing Kansas City's first Cigar Box Guitar Festival—something he'd tried but been unable to get off the ground the previous year.*

Perhaps the most gratifying facet of Kraft's personal cigar box guitar revolution has been what Kevin refers to as therapy-builds. At his day job, Kevin acts as a youth care worker, keeping up with troubled adolescents in an in-patient setting. Drawing on the Bible teaching ministry of radio personality Charles Swindoll, Kraft has developed a presentation in which he assembles a one-string cigar box guitar, or diddley bow, from a collection of apparent junk.

"Chuck Swindoll wrote this thing called Attitude, saying our happiness depends 10 percent on what happens to us and 90 percent on our attitude about it and what we choose to do with it. One of the lines that I keyed in on—he's talking about life, the orchestra that we're all part of, and all we can do is play our one string. So I talk to kids about this whole concept and I start putting it together in front of them. I'm quoting this thing by Chuck Swindoll and by the time I get to the one string part I've got the guitar string and I'm winding it up. By the time I finish the talk, it's a diddley bow. And I start playing it.

I don't know how many kids have left there saying, "Mr. Kevin, that's the best thing I've ever seen—that's the best group I've ever been in." ■

*Author's note: The First Annual KC CBG Festival took place in August 2011 with Kevin at the helm.

## KEVIN KRAFT'S LESSON OF THE DIDDLEY BOW

I usually bring everything—cigar box, wooden dowel or broomstick (prepared), bolts, and a guitar string or wire—in a trash bag, and I sit down before my audience and begin to talk about how trouble and hardship are part of our human existence.

"You may feel like the world is beating you up." I pull out the stick and put it on the floor for them to see. "Or you may feel trapped or boxed into circumstances you can't find your way out of." I set out the box. "People may call you crazy, saying you have a screw loose." I deposit the bolts next to the rest of the items.

"You might think life is just garbage, not unlike these things. Everything you see here is trash. Useless.

"Or is it? I believe attitude is everything. I believe life is what we make of it, and I believe that our attitude is even more important than anything that happens to us.

"Life is like an orchestra in which we all play some part. We can't always stop trouble from entering our lives...all we can do is keep playing. Keep playing the one string we've been given to play." And I pull out the string or wire, and I begin to assemble the diddley bow.

"Because attitude is everything. A man named Charles Swindoll once wrote that he believed life is ten percent what happens to us and ninety percent what our attitude is toward that. It was attitude that caused slaves to survive through the cruelty of slavery to freedom. It is the string of attitude that fuels our self-determination to succeed in the face of failure after failure.

"No matter what happens, a positive attitude makes all the difference." By this time, the diddley bow is completed, strung, and ready to play, and I usually play a tune or a song, and enjoy the look of amazement on the faces of those in my audience."

# THE GODFATHER OF THE CIGAR BOX GUITAR:
# DONALD "BOZ" BOSTWICK
## FLINT, MICHIGAN

*Shane Speal recalls Donald "Boz" Bostwick, who came to be known as The Godfather of the Cigar Box Guitar.*

In the early years of the Cigar Box Guitar Revolution (2003-2005), Donald "Boz" Bostwick was there to support every musician, every builder, and every dreamer. If someone came out with a new model cigar box guitar, Boz would buy one. Record a new CD? Yep, he'd buy the first copy out of the box. He was just excited about the whole movement and wanted to ingest every morsel of homemade goodness.

We started calling Boz "The Godfather of the Cigar Box Guitar."

Donald "Boz" Bostwick was a Vietnam vet who spent the last decades of his life working in the Flint, Michigan auto industry. I met him at the very first Cigar Box Guitar Festival in Carrolton, Kentucky, in 2004. He had driven down from Lapeer, Michigan, on a whim to see what this whole "movement" was about. He later told me that the festival hit him with the intensity and gravity of Woodstock. It radically changed his life.

He became active in our online chat room, signing on nightly to communicate with a group of like-minded musicians and builders. He'd share links to his favorite songwriters such as Warren Zevon and Townes Van Zandt. He'd post pictures of himself holding his latest cigar box guitar acquisitions.

Boz finally got up the courage to take the stage at the 2005 Festival of the Rivers in Hinton, West Virginia. This concert was organized by washboard player Ray Nutter and hosted some of the best cigar box guitar acts known at the time.

**Donald Bostwick.**
The Godfather of the
CIgar Box Guitar.

Boz backing up Gerry Thompson at the 2005 Festival of the Rivers in Hinton, WV.

Boz was to kick off the show. It was his first time on stage.

He took the stage with cigar box guitar builder Kurt Schoen on harmonica and performed songs from his favorite songwriters. He was so nervous his voice was barely a whisper—but it was a start.

Soon after his debut performance, Boz received terrible news from his doctor: He had terminal lung cancer. This sentence hit him just as he was retiring and beginning to discover a whole new musical avenue in life. But the news just became fuel for his fire. Boz had to play more and experience more.

He started buying up more guitars from builders and posting updates on songs he'd been working on. One night, I caught him in the chat room and asked him a simple question, "Have you ever recorded an album?"

"No. I don't have the stuff to do that," he responded.

"Boz, all you need is a simple recorder. Hell, even a tape recorder would work. If you record something, I'll release it on my Insurrection Records label."

He thought about it for a while, but started to go away from the idea until I said, "Everybody always says they want to write a book, but nobody ever sits down to write it. Write the damn book, Boz. Record the album. If this cancer thing is coming after you, then hit back at it by at least recording one album in your life."

That changed everything.

Three weeks later, I received an unmarked envelope in the mail with a CD inside that was marked "Boz: Raw Footage." There was a short note inside:

*Hey Shane,*
*I hope this'll do. Crude. I got drunk and went for it.*

"The thrill of slowly watching a table full of parts turn into a wonderful-sounding instrument is something I think everyone interested in music should experience once, even if they just watch."

**—JULIAN WEAVER, AKA VARNUM SLIM, CIGAR BOX NATION**

The recording opened up with his cover of Warren Zevon's "Don't Let Us Get Sick." Boz changed the words in the last line of the chorus.

*Don't let us get sick*
　　*Don't let us get old*
*Don't let us get stupid, alright?*
　　*Just make us be brave*
*And make us play nice*
　　*And we'll make some music tonight.*

The only sounds were Donald's voice and a Kurt Schoen "Turbodiddley" cigar box guitar. He'd recorded into a single microphone in his kitchen.

Absolute perfection.

By the time I received his recording, Boz was already contemplating more. His first show in West Virginia had been recorded at the soundboard and he was super excited about it. We decided to hand-assemble 50 copies of *Raw Footage* and sell them in order to raise money for a proper release. That release, *Dirty Life and Times*, came out six months later and included his entire set from West Virginia and all the tracks from *Raw Footage*, totally remastered.

Boz opened up the box of freshly printed copies of *Dirty Life and Times*. There it was, his first professional CD. He must have felt like he'd achieved immortality. If he was fired up before, he was in *sonic hyperdrive* now.

Boz at home, playing his four-string cigar box guitar built by Matty Baratto.

PHOTO COURTESY SHANE SPEAL.

Boz went on to self-release five more albums (!), including duet albums with Kurt Schoen (*Drinking Coffee and Staying Up Late*) and Gerry Thompson (*The Last Hard Men*). His songs were also included in the *Masters of the Cigar Box Guitar Vol. III* CD and *Masters Live*.

The Godfather had arrived.

He played his final concert in the early 2007 at the Pix Theater in his hometown of Lapeer, Michigan. It was probably his greatest concert ever...Donald Bostwick's swan song.*

He spent the next couple months at home, playing cigar box guitar. Donald "Boz" Bostwick, The Godfather of the Cigar Box Guitar, passed away on a Sunday morning in September 2007. May he be remembered forever as the Godfather of the Cigar Box Guitar. His love and dedication helped turn this movement into a family.

*—Shane Speal*

*Those archival recordings are streaming at *www.CigarBoxNation.com*. Search "Tribute to Boz Bostwick."

# TED CROCKER
## TALLAHASSEE, FLORIDA

*I called Ted Crocker at his "mad-scientist's laboratory" in southern New Jersey. Working alone from his basement workshop, kept company by his cockatiel, Taxi, Ted uses two Apple computers (connected to three monitors) to oversee both his social network and his custom guitar and component operation.*

*Our conversation got frequent punctuation—Taxi's chirping alternating with the chirping of the "new message" indicator coming from the chat room of his Handmade Music Clubhouse.*

Guitar designer and luthier Ted Crocker grew up in Massapequa, New York, and attended school in nearby Amityville. Yes, *that* Amityville—the one where the movie *The Amityville Horror* takes place. Though he's convinced the notorious hauntings associated with that town were pure fiction, Crocker's own personal horror story (which took place twenty-five years later) was all too real.

On a Wednesday in June of 2004, Crocker stepped on a rusty nail. "Being a typical male, I went inside, washed it, bandaged it with toilet paper and duct tape and went to work the next few days," he reports.

All seemed well until the weekend, when his foot began to look, well, a little puffy.

Ted Crocker was born in 1955 and grew up on Long Island. At age ten, when many Americans were just discovering stereo, Ted had already wired his bedroom for "surround sound," giving new life to fifteen different speakers he'd scavenged from the trash and cast-off television sets. He wired a complex, switched network of speakers to one futuristic looking Panasonic AM/FM/phonograph/cassette player. His system enabled him to put sound in every corner of his bedroom, and then nuance the sound.

"I learned soldering really early," he relates. "My dad was a handyman. He had a lot of tools, did repairs for people as a business. We didn't do projects together, but I learned

**Ted Crocker.** Ted, with his cockatiel, Taxi.

how to use his tools and just made stuff on my own. I was just always making something, or drawing something or writing something. I've always been an inventor, a tinkerer, and I always wanted to play guitar.

"I made my first guitar [when I was] really young, not even a teenager." That first instrument, a guitar-shaped piece of plywood with two strings nailed to it, was a harbinger of things to come, though there would be a few twists in the road before he returned to guitar building.

In high school, Ted's attention turned to muscle cars—tearing them down; building them back up; trying to make his Chevelle Super Sport go faster; trying to avoid getting tickets. He attended college at the State University of New York, then went to DeVry in Phoenix, Arizona, where he studied electronic engineering. In 1978, Crocker returned to New York to look after his ailing mother, who passed away ten years later.

In his early forties, Ted decided it was finally time to learn to play guitar. "I thought, 'I'm old enough, I have some time, I'm really gonna learn.' I'd been wanting to all my life. I wanted to learn to PLAY it, not just pick it up after a few beers and strum along with a CD.

"I bought one at a pawn shop, and it turned out it was a piece of garbage." That might have

**Microwave Dave.**
"Microwave Dave" Gallaher plays a Ted Crocker stereo six-string electric guitar (with both bass and guitar output jacks) on the eve of the 2010 Cigar Box Guitar Extravaganza in Huntsville, Alabama.

been a big disappointment, but when you're Ted Crocker, you don't see things that way. Instead, you rip the guitar apart, salvage parts, and use them to build a new guitar.

Crocker constructed a hollow wooden box shaped like the state of Utah. He attached the salvaged neck and the bridge, wired in the electronics, added an aluminum tray from a TV dinner as an internal resonator, strung it up, and started to play. He calls that one his first "serious" guitar, and he named it The BoSS: "Bo" for Bo Diddley combined with "SS," recalling his speedy Chevelle.

Building the BoSS proved to be a milestone. "I sort of got it then," he says. Crocker found the process of building and playing his own guitar deeply satisfying. He made the rounds with his creation, wanting others to test-drive it, and he got a positive response from just about everyone who played it. He even has a photo of blues legend Pinetop Perkins playing it at the Ft. Lauderdale Blues Festival.

Some old-timers who saw Crocker's BoSS told him it looked like a cigar box guitar. He

got curious and looked up "cigar box guitar" online. "At the time [1998], there was NO information, hardly at all, nothing like what it is today. Somewhere online I saw a picture of one. So I picked up some cigar boxes and started using those."

Ted Crocker had found a new pastime. "I started making cigar box guitars and lap-steels and one-strings. It was really just a hobby. I'd give them away to friends who played."

In 1999, Ted packed up and moved to Florida. "My grandparents and various aunts and uncles had lived there. It was paradise; I loved it. Half my shop was outside." In Florida, Crocker put his electronics education to work, supporting himself by installing home theaters, club lighting, alarm systems, and the like.

In Florida, he also got to be good friends with a musician named Ben Prestage. "He's a one-man-band artist, plays cigar box guitar. With his right foot he plays a bass drum, with his left toe he plays a snare drum and with his heel he plays a cymbal. He's also got a harmonica rack around his neck."

"He's an amazingly talented guy. I'm his biggest fan. I shot photos of him; I put a website together for him; I drove him to some of his gigs when he was having trouble with his van."

Crocker's friendship with Prestage would prove fortuitous. Ben's use of the low-tech cigar box guitar also caught Ted's attention, and further piqued his interest in those instruments.

"In 2003, I stumbled across the Yahoo Cigar Box Guitar group. I think I was the 16th member who joined." Ted became an active part of a growing community. "I seemed to have more experience than anyone. I don't mind helping people out. I enjoy it."

In 2004, though, Ted also stumbled across that rusty nail. After that encounter, he found himself temporarily derailed.

Five days after he stepped on that nail, Crocker came home from work and found he could barely get his boot off. He knew he needed medical attention. Reluctantly, he dragged himself to the hospital ER. "I thought they'd give me a couple of shots and some antibiotics and send me on my way."

The ER doctors had to perform surgery to clean out a deep infection. Though that operation went well, Crocker subsequently contracted MRSA (aka "necrotizing fasciitis", or more commonly, "Flesh Eating Disease").

"They opened up the bottom of my foot to scrape out that infection, but the situation deteriorated. They ended up taking the whole top of my foot off." The entire process involved five separate surgeries, including one last one to graft artificial skin onto the top of his foot.

His hospital ordeal would last a total of three months.

"I'm not someone who's good at sitting down and doing nothing, and all that time in the hospital was, OH GOD, the most boring…"

What's an inveterate tinkerer to do with over fifteen hundred waking hours of hospital time? If you're Ted Crocker, you find an ingenious way to keep in touch with your growing guitar-building fascination.

## "IN 2003, I STUMBLED ACROSS THE YAHOO CIGAR BOX GUITAR GROUP. I THINK I WAS THE 16TH MEMBER WHO JOINED."

"While I was in the hospital in Florida, I had a friend bring by some rolls of Kraft paper. Down in my van I had a Gibson brochure. I had always wanted to build a Flying V and I'd always wanted to build a Gibson Explorer." He adds, "I'm good at math."

Using Gibson's 23¾" (603mm) scale length (distance from bridge to nut), as a reference, Crocker created his own scaled-down ruler. He then applied that to the brochure photos to determine the relative measurements of those legendary Gibson guitars, and folded paper to replicate the angles and each guitar's lines. Scaling everything back up, he transferred drawings to the Kraft paper.

## OVER HIS THREE-MONTH HOSPITAL STAY, CROCKER COVERED THE WALLS OF HIS ROOM WITH HIS DIAGRAMS OF ELECTRIC GUITARS, BECOMING KNOWN AS "THE GUITAR GUY."

"I made full-sized diagrams of those. I made some other full-sized diagrams of other guitars I felt like building." Over his three-month hospital stay, Crocker covered the walls of his room with his diagrams of electric guitars, becoming known as "the guitar guy."

When Ted was finally released from the hospital in September, he entered a world of disability and full-time pain management. The damage wrought by the infections had left him unable to hold a "normal" job. "I tried to get Social Security Disability but I was turned down. I went through the appeals process, but…" By January of 2005, he had run out of money.

## "I BOUGHT A ROUTER TABLE BEFORE I BOUGHT A KITCHEN TABLE."

Out of work, Crocker tinkered in his Florida shop to distract himself from his aching foot. For the next four or five months he worked to hone his guitar-making skills. "When I got out I figured that I'd build something. I found a nice big sheet of luan plywood that had been used to protect the windows of a local tavern during a really rough 2004 hurricane season." Using the patterns he'd made in the hospital and cutting carefully, he used every square inch of that plywood he could.

"I was able to get to Guitar Center, spoke to the repair guy. He sold me a bunch of used parts—some tuners, some pickups, some pots, knobs, and things like that." Crocker managed to make a number of guitars out of that one sheet of wood, but had to keep reusing the same hardware. "I would build a guitar out of luan using those

parts, then take the parts out and use them in another new guitar."

Crocker had made up his mind that he would no longer count on anyone else for a paycheck. In January of 2005, he decided he would try to make a living building guitars. "It was a great hobby, and everybody who'd seen my stuff loved it and said, 'Oh Ted, you should sell these.' So that's what I did."

By February, the financial pressures had become too much. Ted pulled up stakes and left Florida for New Jersey to convalesce at the home of his younger sister. For a little more than half a year, Ted stayed with his sister's family, doing repair work around her house and building cigar box guitars out of the back of his van. "I'd open up the back of my van and pull my very limited tools out. I had a hand drill, a battery-powered circular saw, drill bits, and sandpaper. I was building cigar box guitars, mostly just to keep occupied, but also to learn." He built not only cigar box guitars but also six-string electrics of his own design.

During his convalescence Crocker got more deeply involved in the Internet cigar box guitar building community. The Yahoo group and its offshoot, CIGARBOXGUITARBUILDERS, had been going strong. Ted wanted to create a central clearing house for all things Cigar Box Guitar. "I started Cigar Box Guitar Headquarters on MySpace in June of 07."

"I figured I'd post plans on that blog there, keep posting pictures and things like that, and through the comments people could ask questions and develop a conversation. I thought it was cool to interact with people who were building these things. I really didn't know that anybody else was out there doing anything. Through my efforts and the efforts of Shane Speal, this thing has really grown."

Things soon started to fall into place. Crocker eventually received a lump-sum check from Social Security Disability. "I moved out of my sister's and into a place with a two thousand square-foot basement. I bought a router table

**The Down Under.** No, it's not Australian... This Ted Crocker original is specifically designed for cigar box guitars and meant to drop into a box from the top, so most of the pickup resides "down under" the guitar's sound board.

before I bought a kitchen table. I moved into my shop, spent wisely to get just the tools that I needed." Crocker put together just what he needed to do what he loved—build guitars.

Crocker immediately started into working on one of the high-concept electric guitars he had designed in the hospital, one he called The Taser. "The Taser was the first guitar where I was actually able to buy the parts that I needed. That was a great feeling." When he finished the Taser, he added it on his Ted Crocker MySpace page.

His timing could not have been more fortuitous. Director John Sayles had recently begun preliminary work on a film called *Honeydripper*. Set in the fifties, the film would tell the story of a struggling rural Alabama juke joint. The hero of the film, Sonny, would roll into town playing a crude, handmade electric guitar, and save the day.

The property master for the film lived in South Beach, Florida, and happened to see Ben Prestage playing on the street one night. "He asked Ben if he knew anyone who could build a primitive guitar." Prestage directed the man to Crocker's MySpace page.

"This guy sent me a message and told me what was up. Left his phone number. I immediately called him. I asked him some pointed questions about what he was looking for, the time period, the background of the guy who supposedly built it. That night I got some pictures off to him."

Ted had previously built a guitar he called the Delta Plank. More of a diddley bow, it was just two boards nailed together with some baling wire for strings. "I removed the neck from that and put an old Stella guitar neck on it and I sent him the photos."

Early the next morning, Crocker got a call from the property master. While he admired Ted's enthusiasm, he didn't think Sayles would go for the guitar's shape. An hour later he received a brief email: "John Sayles loves the shape, work up a quote for us."

"That was my break, and that opened up a lot of doors for me. I had to build two guitars and I had two weeks to do it." Those two densely packed weeks would have to accommodate not just building the guitars, but figuring everything out first—including the electronics. "I was driven; I was really driven."

"I had fooled around previously making pickups, but I hadn't used them in any of my builds. I wasn't real comfortable with them, but I had made them. Supposedly this guitar is from 1950, and I guess [Sonny] could have gotten a factory pickup, but I put myself into the mindset of the character in the movie.

"I made up my own little back story to help me with how I was going to build it. My back story was that Sonny was performing in a bar, there was some kind of a fight, his guitar got broken, he was walking home, dejected, along the railroad tracks and found that plank and the rest was history."

According to the screenplay, Sonny had been a communications man in World War Two. To Crocker, that meant Sonny would have known his way around electronics. "I figured that he could possibly find some kind of a coil or a transformer somewhere and turn it into a pickup. So instead of me making a pickup that looked like one you could buy in that day (for serious money back then—this is *early, early* electric guitars), I

**Crocker's Legendary Stonehenge Pickup.** Originally designed for the one-of-a-kind guitar in the movie The Honeydripper, Crocker's Stonehenge line of pickups has become a favorite of electric guitar cognoscenti, including Lenny Robert's Daddy Mojo. The pickups are hand-wound and can be made in everything from single-pole configuration all the way up to six-pole for six-string guitars.

wanted to make it functional but also like it was something that was homemade."

For the *Honeydripper* guitar, Crocker fashioned three separate two-string pickups, designed to sit in a well beneath the strings. He'd later dub this design Stonehenge for the way they looked when lined up together in a photograph.

Ted Crocker's *Honeydripper* guitar fit seamlessly into Sayles period film, becoming a character in its own right, a sort of Best Guitar in a Supporting Role. Crocker's guitar-building enterprise took off almost immediately after the movie.

Crocker travelled to Alabama to attend the 2007 Cigar Box Guitar Extravaganza taking place in Huntsville. At the festival he met Dave "Microwave Dave" Gallaher, a Huntsville blues guitar legend whose band, Microwave Dave and the Nukes, enjoys a solid fan-base, especially in Alabama and Tennessee.

---

## WITH A NOD TO DESTINY, HE'S DUBBED HIS LINE OF PRIMITIVE-CHIC INSTRUMENTS RUSTY NAIL GUITARS.

---

Gallaher wanted Crocker to build him a guitar similar to the Honeydripper, but with a dual output circuit. "I made him a stereo guitar—the bass strings have two sets of pickups and two outputs." This set-up gives Gallaher the option of flipping a switch to feed the lower strings through an octave splitter and a bass amplifier. With this guitar, he can effectively play bass and guitar at the same time.

Within just a few months of creating his MySpace page, Crocker had developed five different custom guitar models, all to fulfill custom orders. "I was building one for Microwave Dave, one for Ben Prestage, another one for a gentleman who found me online, and another one for someone I knew from another blues forum who's a working musician." Crocker's guitars shipped out to rave revues. He soon began to hear from guitar builders, too, who wanted his Stonehenge pickups.

Now Crocker primarily builds high-end guitars and components for professional musicians. He recently built a Honeydripper for platinum-selling country music singer Keith Urban. On a whim, Crocker threw in a three-string calling card: a cigar box guitar he'd built using a tuna can as a resonator.

Crocker has developed a number of other components that have become popular with cigar box guitar builders and musicians. His Tesla Transducer sandwiches a piezo element between two pieces of dense wood, which helps cut down on the piezo's tendency to feed back and transmit sounds made by touching any part of the instrument. His Flatbed integrates the pickup into a bridge and simplifies installation and construction. He's also made a number of turned wood harmonica microphones that fit snugly into the player's palm.

Ted has sold hundreds of the popular and distinctive Stonehenge pickups since opening his own eBay store. In a good month, he'll sell as many as one hundred and fifty of his various pickups. While it takes him about three hours to make a dozen of the cigar box guitar pickups, he builds the Stonehenge pickups strictly on demand, each one hand-wound.

In some ways, he's become a victim of his own success; his component making gets in the way of guitar building. "A lot of times I'll get up in the morning and go down [to the shop] and I've gotta fill six orders and all I want to do is make sawdust on an instrument. At times, this feels like work!"

Ted Crocker's encounter with that rusty nail started him down a path he might not otherwise have taken. The popularity of cigar box guitar building and playing have enabled him to shuck working for others in favor of finding a way to make it on his own as an entrepreneur—in many ways, a dream come true. With a nod to destiny, he's dubbed his line of primitive-chic instruments Rusty Nail Guitars.

Ted Crocker marvels not just at his own success, but at the popularity of instrument building in general. "I don't know if it's the economy, but there are a LOT of people building all kinds of instruments, not just cigar box guitars, instead of sitting in front of the X-Box or TV. I don't think it's just the economy; I think there's a return to the DIY ethic."

"Many of them are older, many are retired. Many have never played a guitar or done any woodworking, but they saw someone playing a cigar box guitar and now that's what they want to do. They start working on one, and next thing you know, they're on number ten. They're learning to play and they're performing. I never would have guessed it would have taken off like this. A lot of credit goes to Shane Speal. He's done a *lot* to promote it, to get the word out."

When Speal discovered the NING social networking platform, a sophisticated, user-friendly, "free-standing" interface, he left Yahoo

## "I THINK THERE'S A RETURN TO THE DIY ETHIC."

and started Cigar Box Nation. Crocker became Cigar Box Nation's member number two and spent a year sharing his expertise and ideas. With his growing interest in six-string guitar design and in building musical instruments other than cigar box guitars, Crocker soon opted to create his own NING community, The Handmade Music Clubhouse. "What I was trying to do there at MySpace is exactly what I'm doing now with the Clubhouse."

"The thing about this whole movement is the spirit of the people, how friendly they are, how willing they are to help, how willing they are to share their 'secrets' with one another. It's not like most other things in life. People here are willing to bend over and let you step on their back so you can get to where you're going." ∎

**Author's note:** July 2011: Ted's packing up his shop in New Jersey to head back south at last. This time he's moving to Tallahassee, Florida—for good. Seems he recently reconnected with a high-school sweetie through Facebook, and she happened to be "single and gorgeous." She still carried a torch for Ted, as well. "I went down there [to Florida] in May [2011] and kissed her for the first time in thirty-seven years." Upon his return to New Jersey, he set about making plans to pack up the shop and move back to Florida, where he studiously avoids stepping on old lumber.

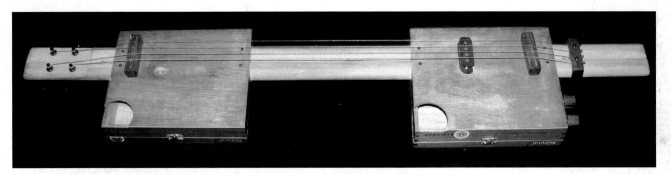

**Lap Dancer.** Crocker built his Lap Dancer to be played lap-steel style. It features a four-pole Stonehenge pickup.

# PAUL BESSETTE
## COCKEYSVILLE, MARYLAND

*Paul Bessette, maker of Uncle Pauly's Boxes, had a vendor's booth at the summer 2010 Cigar Box Guitar Festival in York, PA. We spoke in the cool comfort of the Emporium Book Store.*

"Singing," says artist and musician Paul Bessette, "is how our ancestors expressed joy and sorrow before they developed written language. I think everyone should sing."

Bessette majored in percussion and physics at SUNY, Fredonia. From there, he transferred to Virginia Tech to study aerospace engineering. After living in Virginia for the better part of a decade, he moved to Maryland.

"I worked as an artist the whole time; I never worked as an engineer."

He's also been drumming for close to forty years. As a drummer, he'd been involved with a lot of different bands, covering many styles of music. After decades of backing up punk rockers and metal heads, he finally decided to pursue music that was closer to his heart.

"I grew up on Long Island, living on the water, living on a boat, so I'm kind of an arm-chair whaling historian. I sing sea shanties." Moved by a desire to provide accompaniment for his sea shanties, Paul took guitar lessons for several years, trying to apply that instrument to the style. Ultimately, he decided the guitar was just too much trouble.

Bessette started looking for an instrument that would be easier to play. "So naturally, I landed upon a harmonium. A pump organ. I started researching that, and how much that would cost. It would have been about $200 for a cheap, half-broken used one, or a really crappy one." In addition, he'd have to learn how to play it.

Then Paul stumbled upon cigar box guitars, first on eBay and then on Cigar Box Nation. "I started looking at them. Then I thought about buying one of these things—simplify my whole quest here to have something simple to play just to strum chords behind my sea shanties.

"I'd been working as an artist for over twenty years, I started thinking, I could make that, instead of spending $100–$150 on one I don't even like. So I made one out of all found objects. Eyebolts as tuners. I liked the way it sounded."

**Paul Bessette.** "I think everyone should sing."

"That's how I started making cigar box guitars. I couldn't afford a harmonium. I'm not good enough on the six string. I thought three strings would be easier."

So he made another. This one had a whale carved scrimshaw-style into the back. He called that one a Shanty Box.

"I'm taking this Mississippi Delta slide blues and I'm applying it to Nantucket circa 1838. I'm sure some harpooner had a cigar box guitar at some point."

"So I started building them, and it became this progression. 'Oh, I really like that,' said somebody. 'Oh, I really love this one,' said somebody else. 'How 'bout I buy one off ya?' "You want me to just give it to you?" 'No, no, I couldn't do that. It's too much work. Let me buy it.' "Alright, buy it."

"Then I started selling them for this amount, then for this amount, then people are telling me that I'm not charging enough. My guitars stay in tune. They're extremely durable, as you can see. I build them all by hand, so they've got a lot of soul. And so, that's how I started doing this." ■

# GALLERY: UNUSUAL CBGS

These next few pages highlight some of the more interesting and unique (though every CBG is unique!) instruments I came across while writing this book. Just goes to further show that you can make whatever you want!

**Upright bass by John Nickel.** This two-string bass uses a small cigar box perched atop a microphone stand, which can be disconnected for transport.

**Upright bass, interior.** Interior of bass shows a piezo buzzer and mounting hardware.

**Upright bass, nut.** Here, you can see Nickel's signature coin embedded.

**"Old Lowe" 16" scale CBG with diatonic fretting.** Lowe used red oak for the neck and overlaid a bois d'arc fretboard. He gave this guitar diatonic (dulcimer) fretting and doubled the melody string. The headstock has been adorned with an antique pull-tab.

**"Old Lowe" 16" scale, detail.** The bridge is built from oak and bois d'arc.

**Four-string CBG.** This electric four string was built by John Terrell of Huntsville, Alabama.

**Four-string CBG, tail piece.** Terrell fashioned a string guard out of brushed metal.

**Four-string CBG, back view.** Terrell used recycled lumber for the neck, as evidenced by the old nail hole.

**Four-string CBG, fingerboard inlay detail.** Detail of the mother of pearl inlay work in the fingerboard.

**Papa's Boxes six-string.** Papa's Boxes sells cigar box guitar kits that you can assemble yourself.

**Papa's Boxes six-string, tuners.** Individual tuners are located at the tail end of the guitar.

**Papa's Boxes six-string, headstock.** This kit utilizes simple screws as string anchors.

**Papa's Boxes six-string, back view.** Putting a bracket under the neck provides good support.

**Papa's Boxes six-string, kit.** Here's part of the Papa's Boxes guitar in kit form.

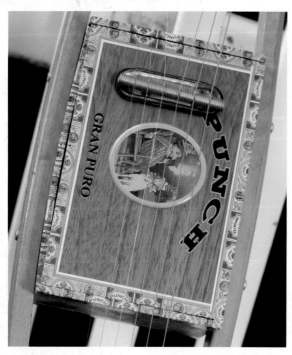

**Crutch six-string CBG, sound box.** Combined threaded rod and a tin lid as a bridge/saddle.

**Crutch six-string CBG, maker's mark.** Madansky's maker's mark.

**Crutch six-string CBG.** Built by Lloyd "Madman" Madansky of Arroyo Grande, California.

**Double-neck harp guitar, detail.** Ballerini selected old-growth cherry milled 50 years ago for the guitar neck and harmonic curve.

**Double-neck harp guitar, saddle/bridge.** The harp guitar combines a six-string guitar and six harp strings.

**Double-neck harp guitar.** Michael Ballerini of Clawson, Michigan built this combination harp/guitar to enter into one of Cigar Box Nation's occasional themed building contests, this one for double-neck guitars.

# JOHN LOWE
## MEMPHIS, TENNESSEE

*I spoke with John Lowe at the Sixth Annual Cigar Box Guitar Extravaganza in Huntsville, Alabama, in June 2010. John was running a booth selling his instruments and also gearing up to play in the concert that night.*

*John sold his first Lowebow at the annual blues festival in Clarksdale, Mississippi, in 1989. Since then, Lowe and his instruments have attained a cult status among blues fans, and he's adopted the Lowebow as his primary instrument.*

You look at John Lowe and you think: Wizard. A lanky six-and-a-half feet tall with long, silvering, wiry hair and piercing blue eyes, it seems all he's missing is a pointy hat and a wand. When you talk to John about his craft, you think: I'm not in Kansas anymore.

"… So I made a steampunk build out of an old Skeletor I had. And it combines the cat-head technology into the Hill Harp, where you can squeeze the necks and change the tone. My ideas are always cross-pollinating and coming up with new permutations."

Indeed. John's legendary Lowebows and Hill Harps draw from eclectic sources (both material and spiritual), becoming powerful musical assemblages of seemingly unrelated parts: oak dowels, hose clamps, sewing machine bobbins, cigar boxes, tin cans, bicycle inner tubes, and titanium—the list keeps growing because John's curiosity and capacity for innovation appear to be inexhaustible.

Lowe's instruments continue to evolve with each build, which makes defining the Lowebow like trying to map a sand dune. It's as if John took the guitar back to its most primal origins and has been guiding it along an evolutionary path—one parallel to, but divergent from, that of the conventional guitar. His instruments bring their own mythology in tow.

John's interest in music started early. An uncle exposed him to boogie-woogie piano playing, and piano lessons began at age four. As John tells it, "I was always banging on my rich grandpa's Steinway when I would visit him out on his Red River plantation. I didn't last long in piano—the teacher wanted me to play middle C most of the lesson … that was more than I could handle."

"I had trumpet lessons for about six weeks in fourth grade, but then, when I was fifteen, I got a Sears Silvertone guitar for Christmas." The Sears guitar lost out two years later to a 1959 Les Paul Junior. "Then I actually started making progress because I had something I could play."

Other than a few casual lessons in Austin "from this guy who supposedly played with Frank Zappa," John learned to play guitar primarily from jamming with friends. He formed numerous bands, played in clubs in the 80s, and was very active in the somewhat-legendary Fayetteville, Arkansas punk scene in 1984 and 1985.

When John and his wife, Bev, lived in Fayetteville, they had a little music store called Rock House Music. In response to his wife's "wanderlust," they packed Rock House into boxes and moved on to Santa Rosa, California. Soon after that, they landed back in Bev's hometown of Memphis, Tennessee, where they live today.

**John Lowe.** John Lowe at the Steel Bridge Songfest in Sturgeon Bay, Wisconsin.

## JOHN'S CURIOSITY AND CAPACITY FOR INNOVATION APPEAR TO BE INEXHAUSTIBLE.

**Lowebow.** Double-neck cigar box bass/guitar built by John Lowe of Memphis, Tennessee, and owned by Bill Jehle.

In Memphis, they opened Xanadu Bookstore in 1983. In 1986, they took the remains of Rock House Music out of storage, and Xanadu Bookstore became Xanadu Books and Music. Significantly, the name has once again been updated, this time to Xanadu Music and Books.

One fateful day, Old Miss grad student Jay Kirgis walked into Xanadu and asked John if he knew where he could get a magnetic pickup for a single-string. Kirgis was at work on a graduate thesis that involved the diddley bow*. He'd built a number of fine-art, cigar-box-based diddley bows and wanted to amplify them. As luck would have it, another Xanadu customer had recently talked to John about building one-string pickups using sewing machine bobbins, copper wire, and cylindrical magnets. Lowe told Kirgis to check back in a week and he'd have one ready.

The pickups worked well. Later, Jay Kirgis left a couple of his amplified diddley bows at Xanadu on consignment. Though those instruments did not sell, they did leave an impression on the shop's owner. In his down time at Xanadu, John experimented with playing one of Kirgis' creations and feeding it back through the big Orange amplifiers he had in the store inventory. "I was kind of into Hendrix, making all that feedback noise."

He liked the sound.

John says his wife, Bev, couldn't stand retail, and knowing John was good with his hands, had recently been encouraging him to "make something." Inspired by Jay Kirgis' diddley bows and the electric pickups they'd developed, Lowe started building one- and two-string "stick guitars"—using just a dowel, hose clamps, a copper coupling, and his own homemade pickups. Respectful of Jay's work (and his own creative process), John added his own twist by leaving out the cigar box—its resonating properties lost importance when the electric pickup was introduced. His stick guitars resembled broom handles with taut wires stretched from end to end.

Lowe had been playing his stick guitars, alternately referred to as harps, for over a year when bluesman Richard Johnston stopped in to Xanadu. Johnston loved Lowe's stick guitar and asked John to build him one with a cigar box as a resonating chamber for acoustic play. The box would also make the instrument easier to handle—as John admits, "the stick kind of rolls around in your hand."

---

## JOHNSTON LOVED LOWE'S STICK GUITAR AND ASKED JOHN TO BUILD HIM ONE WITH A CIGAR BOX AS A RESONATING CHAMBER FOR ACOUSTIC PLAY.

---

That encounter started John Lowe down another path. As he reported to Shane Speal: "I made an acoustic called Angelic Acoustic and also a Helltone electric model. Richard Johnston wanted an electric/acoustic, so his first was a three string we called Purgatory. He fell in love with it and took it everywhere with him." Later, Lowe showed Johnston a double-neck model with an additional separate neck for a bass string. "Richard saw that and told me to move the necks together so he could play bass and guitar at the same time. I made one and we called it the Purgatory Hill Harp; "Purgatory" being somewhere between the angels and hell, and "hill," a tribute to a style of blues originating in the hill country of north Mississippi.**

The ultra-earthy slide sounds of the Hill Harp combined with Johnston's lush, rich blues vocals would prove unstoppable. Just one week after he took possession of the new Purgatory Hill

---

* An ethnomusicologist would formally call it a "monocord zither." See: David Williams.

** From the Web site Mississippi Blues Trail: "In the greater Holly Springs area, musicians developed a 'hill country' blues style characterized by few chord changes, unconventional song structures, and an emphasis on the "groove" or a steady, driving rhythm. In the 1990s, this style was popularized through the recordings of local musicians R.L. Burnside and David 'Junior' Kimbrough."

Harp, Richard Johnston shocked the blues world by winning The Blues Foundation's 17th-Annual International Blues Challenge in Memphis. It was the first time anyone had won both first place and the Albert King Award, and the first time anyone had won playing a cigar box instrument.

## THE ONE-MAN-BAND FORCED ME TO THINK ABOUT THE WHOLE SONG.

Richard Johnston reigned at the Blues Challenge using a one-man band format. He played a high-hat and a whole bunch of drums with his feet while managing both guitar and bass lines with his new Lowebow.

John Lowe soon adopted the one-man-band format, too—John plays an additional drum using a drumstick clutched in his strumming hand. He started getting out to play more—with Johnston, Robert Belfour, and others, working his way through a series of both club and busking

**Lowebow, tail.** Detail of tail end and string anchors. Lowe uses bottlecaps to keep the strings from tearing into the wood.

settings on and off Memphis' legendary Beale Street. John started touring a bit, playing the Cat Head in Clarksdale, Mississippi, the King Biscuit in Houston, Texas, and the Uno-A-Go-Go one-man-band show in Chicago.

"The one-man-band thing saved me because I was a self-indulged musician and I overplayed. I could not get an audience because it was 'over-evolved'; I was shreddin' all the time and nobody wanted to hear it. The one-man-band forced me to think about the whole song. If you're going to play three parts, you can't shred. It also gave me a physical activity that was meaningful. I was overweight, and it got me in condition. The instruments saved my business because now I had something people couldn't buy at the big megastore."

An Internet community had meanwhile grown up around the building and playing of cigar box guitars. John got involved. When the first CBG festival took place in Carrollton, Kentucky, in 2006, he performed there, and later at the Festival of the Rivers in Hinton, West Virginia. "During my Beale Street playing, Matt Crunk saw me, and he organized this festival [The Annual Cigar Box Guitar Extravaganza in Huntsville, Alabama] for me because he wanted to do something for me."

Through life's ups, downs, and curves, John continues to follow the paths that open to him. He puts a lot of trust in his own unique creative process and clearly embraces uncertainty. "The thing is, I DON'T KNOW WHAT I DO. Tonight? I don't know what I'm gonna play. Inspiration comes through you. I believe in surreal expression—it comes through you; it comes from your subconscious.

"Sure, I'd like to think that I thought this stuff up one morning and drew up some plans and built it, but a lot of my design things were mistakes. That's why I don't want to stick with any one design, because I might make another good mistake. The hardest part is creating something that's simple. Everybody wants to make things complex."

The demand for Lowe's innovatively simple instruments has grown, and now John divides his time between building Lowebows and playing them. "Yes, I'm trying to make money, but I don't want to see them mass-produced in China or anything."

Still, his success hasn't come without the occasional frustration. "You'll have Richard [Johnston] up there just kickin' butt on my instrument and some guy says, 'That sounds better than my ten thousand dollar–rig'. Some jerk will then get on a chat room and say, 'That's just twenty dollars worth of stuff; it's just sewing machine bobbins.' There's a *little* bit of craft involved (and it's a little more than twenty-dollar's-worth of materials, just for the record). I don't know why people are so mean, always tryin' to belittle things, you know. It's more than the sum of its parts. If you look at a Les Paul, you can say that's just $350-worth of materials in a twenty thousand dollar–guitar—it's the way that it's put together, the thought and the time, and the years of experience."

And maybe just a touch of wizardry. Lowebows have also found their way into the hands of Lyle Lovett, Harry Manx, members of the North Mississippi Allstars, and other notables. "It's all goin' real good for me. I've had pat mAcdonald playing my instruments and I've been going up to his [Steel Bridge] festivals for three years now; Ben Prestage is going all over the world playing them; of course (Huntsville, Alabama's) Microwave Dave, John Alex Mason, and Keyan Williams.

"What makes my instruments valuable is the sound. It's also that there's artist association with me—just like a Gibson. The Chinese can

**Lowebow, headstock.**
A single piece of composite spans both necks, providing a string nut for both guitar and bass sides.

make a guitar probably better than a lot of the Gibsons now, but they don't get the same money for them 'cause they're not the artist."

John's blue eyes pick up a new intensity. His wiry wizard's hair bounces as he bobs his head for emphasis. "I think what Richard and I have done is really meaningful. He's like Elvis in a way. He created a new format and music needs new formats, otherwise it's stale. You can only change formats by having new machinery. You can only move forward by going back." ∎

## "WHAT MAKES MY INSTRUMENTS VALUABLE IS THE SOUND."

# RICHARD JOHNSTON
## MEMPHIS, TENNESSEE

*I spoke with Richard Johnston by phone as he enjoyed a mild, sunny, mid-winter Saturday with friends in Arkansas. He'd gone to Arkansas to contemplate his next move. An unexpected change in Beale Street's economic and political climate ("It's become the home of dance music rather than blues, partly due to the drop-off in tourist traffic") had forced Johnston off the lip of the street where he'd been busking for tips in front of The New Daisy Theatre for the better part of a decade.*

*At the time of this writing, he's lined up to return to the Black Diamond, where he started his tenure on Beale Street over ten years ago. Johnston calls the Black Diamond, owned by his original Memphis benefactor, Bob Harding (and situated just out of reach of the loudspeakers blasting dance music), "one of the last legitimate blues clubs on Beale Street."*

 "Playing trance hill country music on Beale Street on diddley bows was just about the best. There was no better place for me to be with my style of music, outside of a North Mississippi juke joint."

As a boy, Richard Johnston developed an affinity for playing droning, repetitive guitar music. He'd been given what he calls "a four-string six-string guitar," a standard guitar missing two strings, when he was ten. "While I didn't know how to play chords," he says, "I liked to drone on the guitar. As far back as I can remember, 1975, I was picking two strings on an instrument, finding the octave, and droning. For hours."

After years of playing a variety of music, from rock and roll to country, Johnston would embrace that droning sound again, and ride it to win the Blues Society's International Blues Challenge as a one-man-band—featuring a cigar box guitar.

**Richard Johnston.**
Richard Johnston and one
of his many Lowebows.

**The original.** This is the original John Lowe/ Richard Johnston collaboration instrument that Johnston played to sweep the Blues Society's International Blues Challenge in 2001.

2011 JAKE HERRLE

"PLAYING TRANCE HILL COUNTRY MUSIC ON BEALE STREET ON DIDDLEY BOWS WAS JUST ABOUT THE BEST. THERE WAS NO BETTER PLACE FOR ME TO BE WITH MY STYLE OF MUSIC, OUTSIDE OF A NORTH MISSISSIPPI JUKE JOINT."

When Johnston headed to San Diego State University to study industrial sociology and philosophy, he naturally took a guitar (with all six strings) along with him. At SDSU, one of his fellow students introduced him to the music of Robert Johnson, and Johnston was hooked. "I was twenty-five years old when I heard the open-G stylings of Robert Johnson. It just kind of blew my mind."

Through San Diego State's Asia Pacific exchange program, Johnston headed off to Japan for a year of study at Gifu University. In Japan, Johnston dove so deeply into Robert Johnson that other students in his dormitory (who'd evidently heard enough) politely suggested Johnston try out a venue other than his dorm room.

Johnston took his guitar down to a local watering hole called The Beer Hall, and there became a Wednesday night fixture strumming his newfound open-G tunes for free beers.

He couldn't have known it at the time, but those students who drove him out of his dorm room were instrumental in transforming Johnston's one-year Japan term into a five-year stay, which would encompass not just a year of study, but a three-year marriage, four years as a professional musician, and an all-around change in life-direction.

As he tells it, "Someone from a bigger town saw me on a Wednesday night and hired me, and that was my first paying gig—at a place called Santa Barbara in a Mexican-style foreign bar in Nagoya, Japan.

"I'd get on a train, they gave me a hotel room, and I'd get two hundred bucks to play my country blues. I'd been so poor as a student; I had never seen money like that before in a day. I couldn't believe it, and so I continued to do it as a part-time job as I went to school."

Performing music soon won out over academics. Johnston's rich, soulful vocal style and developing guitar sound proved popular—and marketable. "I was smart enough to see that I had worked hard to go to school and if I were going to go to grad school it was going to take more money, more investment. I decided not to; I decided to play music. I just loved it; I enjoyed it. It made me feel OK. Everything I'd studied in San Diego had just alarmed me about the world. The more you read about what's going on the more alarmed you'll get. Maybe I put my head in the sand a little bit, but the music brought me back to just feeling all right."

Four years into his new career, Bill Ellis, a writer for the *Memphis Commercial Appeal*, caught Johnston's act in Nagoya. When Ellis returned home, he suggested Johnston for a Memphis music festival called Bluestock. Ellis later phoned Johnston from Memphis to ask if he'd like to participate.

"He said, 'Richard? I'm writing for the *Commercial Appeal* and they've got a festival coming up and I suggested you for the line-up.' I got my first festival gig after four years of what turned out to be regional playing in Japan. I went on from that to my first festival in Memphis in 1997."

On his visit to Memphis, Richard Johnston got his first taste of Beale Street's irresistible charms. "I enjoyed Beale Street, I enjoyed being near it, and I decided to return." Four months after Bluestock, Johnston left Japan to live in Memphis.

## RELOCATING TO MEMPHIS, SO NEAR THE HILL COUNTRY OF NORTH MISSISSIPPI, WOULD STRONGLY INFLUENCE JOHNSTON'S MUSICAL DIRECTION.

Johnston found he could support himself busking on Beale Street. "It was a good living. In Japan, I had moved up to the three-to five-hundred-dollars-a-show category, working four or five nights a week, and I was making a pretty good living out there." He may not have earned as much on Beale Street, but, he says, "gas prices were cheaper, rent was cheaper, everything was cheap, cheap, cheap in Memphis, and the economy was still pretty good back in the late nineties and early turn of the millennium."

Relocating to Memphis, so near the Hill Country of North Mississippi, would strongly influence Johnston's musical direction. He had first listened to Hill Country Blues in Japan. "I knew about R.L. Burnside, but I'd never heard of Junior Kimbrough. There was only so much country blues out there. Playing it was fun, so I was learning how to do it and busking for tips on Beale Street in 1998." Then Johnston discovered Junior Kimbrough's music. "There's a big difference between Robert Johnson and Junior Kimbrough. That's where the next stage began, when I hit Beale Street and was playing mainly a repertoire of Hill Country music."

"In fact, when I came to do that show from Japan [in 1997], I was on the bill with Junior Kimbrough. I opened for him that night, and he didn't show up. I had asked Bill Ellis, 'Who's this Junior Kimbrough? I like that name; that's cool; who is he?' He died the following year."

---

## JOHNSTON WALKED INTO JOHN LOWE'S XANADU MUSIC AND BOOKS IN 2001 AND SAW JOHN LOWE'S EXPERIMENTAL, HANDMADE CIGAR BOX GUITARS FOR THE FIRST TIME.

---

Since 1992, Junior Kimbrough had operated a popular juke joint in Chulohoma, Mississippi, called Junior's Place. Kimbrough's band played Hill Country Blues at Junior's Place every Sunday night and attracted visitors from around the world, including Keith Richards, members of U2, and Iggy Pop. "He started to tell me the story and I was like LET'S GO. Junior didn't show up that night, either; he was ill toward the end."

Johnston's friend, guitarist Mark Simpson, gave Richard a stack of Junior Kimbrough cassettes to listen to. Though Johnston never would meet Kimbrough nor hear him play (Kimbrough died in early 1998), Kimbrough's music and legacy would become a major influence in Johnston's music and career.

It turns out Johnston had recently been thinking about starting a band. In mid-1998, he and Simpson called Kinney Kimbrough (Junior's son) and Garry Burnside (R.L. Burnside's son), who had been Junior's band at the time he died. Johnston simply asked if they wanted to continue doing Junior's music.

"Kinney told me, 'Yeah, I'll be in a band with you man, but you've gotta come to the juke joint every Sunday night. I don't care if we're in France, you gotta be back on Sunday. At the juke joint you get twenty-five bucks, a chicken sandwich

(with the bones still in) and all the beer you can drink.'" He quickly agreed to the terms and he, Kinney Kimbrough, Garry Burnside, and Mark Simpson became the Soul Blues Boys, playing at Junior's Place every Sunday night.

The band broke up, though, when Junior's Place burned to the ground in April of 2000. The fire at the juke joint completely leveled the club. Johnston lost all of his gear in the fire. "They did some kind of a fundraiser and I ended up getting a guitar and an amp back, but it wasn't what I'd lost.

"I got this Johnson; a really cheap Dobro. It was a wooden bodied sort of slim-lined Dobro that fit on your lap like a regular acoustic guitar would. I ended up putting a scratch plate on it and putting a mic on there and would scratch on my scratch plate and strum on my dobro at the same time while I played the drums with my feet."

Johnston returned to busking on Beale. "That's what I was doing when I met John Lowe."

Still not satisfied with his replacement gear, Johnston walked into John Lowe's Xanadu Music and Books in 2001 and saw John Lowe's experimental, handmade stick guitars for the first time.

"I play slide, so I always have a slide with me. I said, 'Oooo, can I listen to that?' I plugged it in and MAN, John had made a monster. It was a one-string bass I think. He let me play a two-string guitar, too."

Johnston wanted one. He discussed his needs with Lowe, who then built Johnston his first cigar box guitar. "The first thing he made for me was a three-string single-neck. We worked a little bit on pickup placement and stuff like that. I still have that guitar."

Johnston admits he had floundered for about a year after Junior's Place burned down, but "I made a move when I found John. I'd entered a blues competition [the Blues Foundation's International Blues Challenge (IBC)] 'cause I didn't have anything else to do with my time besides go back to Beale Street and busk."

"John was making cigar box guitars and I asked him to customize one. I said, look, I play drums with my feet now and guitar, why can't I play bass? If you make me a cigar box guitar that has a guitar and a bass right next to each other... John said, 'Well, that's a stupid idea. Why would you want to do that?' I thought, 'Well, you'll see.' He said, 'That's a dumb idea. You'll need two amps!' And I said, 'Exactly.'"

"About a month after I asked him for the [double-neck] guitar, he finally gave me the first prototype. He really resisted the idea of putting the necks together, like right next to each other, so he put them two inches apart." Johnston didn't have a guitar slide that would cover that distance. "I had to get a plumber's pipe and cut it off—like my middle finger was six inches long—to play the thing, but it did what I asked."

Lowe wired the prototype double-neck cigar box guitar/bass with separate outputs for the bass and guitar. "I could play them. They were set to scale so when I moved the slide up, they functioned together. So I started lugging all this stuff around with me just to play maybe two songs on this cigar box guitar."

The new, collaboratively designed instrument actually combined two of Lowe's previous guitar concepts—a bass he'd named the Helltone model and a guitar he'd called the Angelic Acoustic. He saw this new instrument as something in between, so with a nod toward the North Mississippi Hill Country, Richard and John dubbed it the Purgatory Hill Harp.

Johnston had entered the IBC as a solo act, competing against over a thousand bands from around the world. He'd made it into the semi-finals "just with a Dobro, a regular acoustic guitar, and an old Sears Silvertone. I made it on three guitars, just sittin' up there, playin' slide and singin.'"

**Arturo Fuente.** One of Richard Johnston's most heavily used Lowebow guitars.

2011 JAKE HERRLE

**Arturo Fuente, tail view.**
Tail view, showing the bass and guitar string ends and dual audio output jacks.

"As the finals approached, I asked the people, 'Can I change the instrument I play?' They said, 'We don't care, as long as there's not another person on stage that wasn't there the day that you won your heat.'"

When he got to the finals, Johnston came out as a one-man band for the first time in his life, wielding his new Purgatory Hill Harp. "I was playing a high-hat with my heel, a snare with my left toe, a kick drum…I had a bass, I had a three-string, and I was singin' my ass off."

When all the smoke he'd made finally cleared, Johnston found he'd not only won first prize in the international competition, he'd also been awarded the coveted Albert King Guitar Award.

"I got out there and I won the whole thing. It blew us all away. John and I were SO excited that that new instrument had done that right out of the chute, you know, international competition. It was GREAT. Then he went back and built me one that I could actually play!"

Johnston ponders the incineration of his gear, his meeting John Lowe, the development of the Purgatory Hill Harp, and sweeping the International Blues Challenge.

"It was a real comedy of errors to meet John, and to get to know him. The Hill Harp came out of it and it changed my life and changed his."

He finds the Purgatory Hill Harp ideally suited to Hill Country Blues. "Hill country blues—they've been known to stay on the 'One.' It's the one style of music in all of blues where

> **WHEN ALL THE SMOKE HE'D MADE FINALLY CLEARED, JOHNSTON FOUND HE'D NOT ONLY WON FIRST PRIZE IN THE INTERNATIONAL COMPETITION, HE'D ALSO BEEN AWARDED THE COVETED ALBERT KING GUITAR AWARD.**

they don't have song structure; they'll just start a rhythm and stay on it—they don't make a chord change. So it was a perfect instrument to play hill country blues on, that's for sure."

Johnston notes that working with his Purgatory Hill Harp has influenced his guitar playing as well. "Once you start you develop a style on your cigar box and then you go back and play your regular guitar, it makes you play that differently. It's a skill set you get, and then when you apply that to playing on your six-string fretted instrument, it has a huge impact on that as well."

Guitar players who move to the cigar box guitar reap another reward as well, according to Johnston. "You HAVE to learn how to play the slide. That's another thing that a six-string guitar doesn't usually presuppose, that you're going to have to learn to play slide. But one of these cigar boxes, unless they're fretted, 99% of the time somebody's got a slide on their hand. It's a great instrument for that reason; it kind of demands you to put a slide on your finger.

"The other part about it that's just amazing," he goes on, "I gotta say, if they're built right—and not all of them are—if you get a hot cigar box in your hand, there's just something earthy about it. You don't really need to play a song, it's like hearing a note over and over again…it's a *good* thing, a good solid note. Ahhhhhh. If they're built right, they're just beautiful, too.

"What I think is interesting is that at a time when the economy is going bad, a found object artist makes something and I come along and maybe modify it and make this very appealing model of it…it's beyond something that makes a song, when you start to think of the art of it, you start to think of its historical significance and you start to realize music is more than that.

"It's not just about a song. So many people are making 'em now. It brings you back, as John put it, to found object art. Taking things that were lying around and making something so powerful and inventive as he did. It's social context."

## "IT WAS A REAL COMEDY OF ERRORS TO MEET JOHN, AND TO GET TO KNOW HIM. THE HILL HARP CAME OUT OF IT AND IT CHANGED MY LIFE AND CHANGED HIS."

"We got lucky with the Hill Harp. The Hill Harp pretty much does it. It's in its most usable form right now. It is a new instrument. It is as definitive to me as a VIOLIN or a BANJO. It is indeed a *new* instrument."

For Johnston, the cigar box guitar experience goes beyond the instrument, even beyond the music. "It's just not one level. It's not just one thing that happened. We didn't just get a cool-sounding guitar out of it; we got a lot more than that. We got a whole new world of friends and a whole lot of weird things that have happened. It's magical.

"I've gone on from that to do thirteen countries and play hill country blues at some of the biggest festivals in the world, and I've had a really good time doin' it." ■

**Arturo Fuente, face.** Johnston's Arturo Fuente Lowebow has a face like an ancient, well-traveled blues man.

# PAT MACDONALD
## STURGEON BAY, WISCONSIN

*Most famous as singer, guitarist, and main songwriter for Timbuk3 (which scored a 1986 top-20 hit with their catchy "The Future's So Bright, I Gotta Wear Shades"), pat mAcdonald is now half of the duo Purgatory Hill. He's also co-founder of the Steel Bridge Songfest, an annual not-for-profit benefit concert held in his current hometown of Sturgeon Bay, Wisconsin. I spoke with pat mAcdonald at The Emporium Book Store, shortly after Purgatory finished their energetic set at the 2010 York, Pennsylvania, Cigar Box Guitar Festival.*

*The big, integrated, driving Purgatory Hill sound, with its fat bass line, complex sliding guitar, and stripped-down rhythms still resonated in my ears and abdomen as we retreated to the bookstore's office, which served as the Green Room for the show. After pat had recharged himself with some brownies and graciously extended himself to a number of fans and friends, we settled into a long chat about the evolution of his musical style and his cigar box guitar's place in that evolution.*

*David Sutton*

"It does surprise me that it came so naturally and so inevitably, that, at this point in my life, I'd take up a whole different instrument and a different sound."

That's singer/songwriter/Grammy nominee pat mAcdonald, talking about an instrument he lovingly refers to as "That Thing."

The sound pat's referring to? That's the sound he gets from "That Thing"—a John Lowe cigar-box-based creation called the Purgatory Hill Harp. pat had been chasing that sound like an acoustical Holy Grail for years, trying to wring it out of his six-string Chet Atkins electro-acoustic guitar. His album, *Troubadour of Stomp*, represents the culmination of his efforts to attain that sound using a conventional six-stringed guitar.

With all due respect to his guitars, mAcdonald had long been tuning the instruments way down from standard tuning. "Sometimes I even tuned the bass string [E in standard tuning] to B-flat, which is pretty low for a regular guitar."

In pursuit of his "Holy Grail" sound, mAcdonald had split the output of his guitar into two signals with a Y-cable, separating the sound into two paths. He sent one signal, unadulterated, straight through to his sub-woofer. He sent the other through his distortion pedals and guitar amp. "That's the one that gets compressed and messed with," mAcdonald explains.

pAt macdonald had been playing and touring solo since 1995, writing prolifically and developing a complex, sophisticated one-man-band act with a surprisingly massive sound. One night in 2006, during a break in a show at San Francisco's Café du Nord, a fan showed him an odd-looking instrument. "He asked me if I thought it was cool."

Lloyd Cole had bought the instrument, a cigar box guitar creation called a Purgatory Hill Harp, from instrument builder John Lowe in Memphis. Cole tried it out but didn't really take to the instrument. pat didn't know it at the time, but Cole planned to pass the instrument on to him if pat liked it. He accepted Cole's generous offer and took the instrument on the road with him.

**pat mAcdonald.**
pat mAcdonald and his Purgatory Hill Harp at the 2010 York, Pennsylvania, Cigar Box Guitar Festival.

**Purgatory Hill.** melaniejane and pat mAcdonald rest up in the Emporium Bookstore in York, Pennsylvania, after headlining the 2010 York CBG Festival.

The Purgatory Hill Harp had two necks made from one-inch oak dowels. The upper neck supported a bass guitar string and the lower neck, three guitar strings.

"I thought it was cool; it seemed a novelty instrument at the time because I didn't plug it in. It had a pretty nice sound acoustically, but I had never played a slide before so there was very little I could do on it."

## IT WAS AS IF SOMEONE HAD SLIPPED THE HOLY GRAIL INTO THIS KNIGHT'S SADDLEBAGS WITHOUT TELLING HIM.

Still, mAcdonald found "That Thing" intriguing to play. The harp was tuned to an open E [E–E–B–E]. He found he could press the bass string and the middle of the three guitar strings against their respective oak dowels to create different notes, but the first and third guitar strings were too far away from the surface to make contact with those. "The only thing I could figure out how to play [without a slide] was a weird version of 'Baby Please Don't Go.'" pat contented himself with that for a week or so, and otherwise enjoyed noodling around with his new, "novelty" instrument.

Then, one night in Portland, Oregon, musical lightning struck.

mAcdonald arrived in Portland for a gig at Devil's Point, a little strip club/rock bar. "I was pulling up to Devil's Point to play my gig. I knew these guys in Portland. It turns out they're cigar box guitar enthusiasts, and I told them I'd gotten this "thing." They asked to see it, and when they saw it they were like, 'Whoa, man! Johnny Lowebow made that! You really have somethin' there. That guy bought that for you? He paid some money for that, that's not a toy!'"

Then they asked the million-dollar question: Had he plugged it in? "I said no ... they said, 'You gotta plug it in, man'". So pat took it inside with him, and during sound check, he plugged it in.

"You ask, when did I become hooked on the Lowebow? The instant I plugged it in and heard what it sounded like amplified. It's an amazing sound amplified; it's a totally different animal when you plug it in."

It was as if someone had slipped the Holy Grail into this knight's saddlebags without telling him. "I knew that I had to work with it and find my way around it. I knew that I was going to be using it. It's perfectly made for my style of picking."

pat's left handed, but he'd learned to play guitar the way a right hander does (the guitar he learned on was his mother's, so restringing it was never an option). Turning the instrument upside-down never occurred to him. "In a way it's always been a handicap." Right-hand finger-picking patterns, for example, required a lot of practice and patience. "In another way, it's evolved into a stylistic element."

The John Lowe creation suited pat's picking style. "It has the bass string for my thumb and the three guitar strings to correspond with my three picking fingers." He uses that finger-picking configuration for a lot of his playing, but he can also do "more strummy things. I do this strum on the bass string alone sometimes, like I'm holding a pick in my hand. I use my pointer fingernail to strum the bass string back and forth."

Lloyd Cole had also given pat a little medicine-bottle slide that pat didn't like very much. Learning to play with a slide, though, meant he could play his Hill Harp in keys other than E just by starting with the slide in different positions. "I started doing this thing with starting on what you'd call the second fret, or F#. I liked that 'cause then you could go down to the E from there. I like the F# position on the Lowebow. So I was playing around with starting in the F# position and what came out of that was 'Reset Me Lord,' the first song I wrote on that instrument."

While playing with a slide, pat's left-handedness turned to an advantage. "My *smart* hand is the one with the slide, which is the opposite of a lot of people who play slide. I think I get a lot more feel, more vibe, and maybe even more precision from the slide; an almost unconscious connection with the notes without having to think too much."

pat eventually got a heavy ceramic slide, which he says made all the difference. "Suddenly the guitar, the THING, came alive. With the ceramic slide…" mAcdonald draws a dramatic breath and lets out a low whistle.

---

## "I THINK I GET A LOT MORE FEEL, MORE VIBE, AND MAYBE EVEN MORE PRECISION FROM THE SLIDE; AN ALMOST UNCONSCIOUS CONNECTION WITH THE NOTES WITHOUT HAVING TO THINK TOO MUCH."

---

The Purgatory Hill Harp's bass string and John Lowe's hand-wound pickups gave pat mAcdonld the low-end he'd been trying for so long to squeeze out of his guitar. The Lowebow is built with two separate outputs, one for the pickup dedicated to the bass string, and the other serving the two pickups that cover the three guitar strings. That configuration allows him to amplify and process the lows and the highs differently, as he'd been doing using a Y-cable with his guitars.

mAcdonald had been content playing live as a one-man-band, but he'd felt he needed some hand percussion—shaker and tambourine—and backing vocals. For his albums *In The Red Room* and *Troubadour of Stomp* pat says he ended up overdubbing the hand percussion, "and I'd just sing my own backups, just a few little light harmonies. *Troubadour of Stomp* had that. But I couldn't reproduce it live."

Back in 2002, pat had met singer/songwriter/multi-instrumentalist melaniejane, who had been making waves with her songwriting and her electric cello. mAcdonald had always been a fan of the cello, and melaniejane plays a low,

## THE PURGATORY HILL HARP'S BASS STRING AND JOHN LOWE'S HAND-WOUND PICKUPS GAVE PAT MACDONLD THE LOW-END HE'D BEEN TRYING FOR SO LONG TO SQUEEZE OUT OF HIS GUITAR.

**Purgatory Hill harp.**
Tail view detail, showing the jacks.

rocking cello, "kind of edgy and fat," that went well with his deep guitar sound. By 2007, they'd started performing together.

In addition to performing her own music, melaniejane was taking on those things pat felt had been lacking in his one-man-band configuration. The two performers developed into a duo with pat playing guitar and melaniejane adding backup vocals and switching off between cello and hand percussion.

Eventually, the list of songs pat had written around the Purgatory Hill Harp developed into a set. When he'd take out his cigar box guitar, he says, "We'd switch to another configuration, like it was another band." Gradually, more of their set centered on songs pat had written around the Purgatory Hill Harp. Before long, that part of their act became the dominant set. "We started doing some shows where, if we were only playing an hour or so, we would do all cigar box. Now a lot of people have never heard melaniejane play the cello. They've heard the Purgatory Hill thing but they haven't heard the other thing."

2008 rolled around and mAcdonald still didn't know who John Lowe was. He'd been playing "that thing" for nearly two years, even toyed with the idea of adopting the name Purgatory Hill as a "blues pseudonym", but still had no idea where the name "Purgatory Hill Harp" came from. "I did want to find out, though."

"In my audacity, I thought, I'm playing this thing called a Purgatory Hill Harp. I'm going to imagine this thing was made for me and I'm PURGATORY HILL."

pat hoped the Harp's creator would not be too annoyed. Once he'd recorded a couple of songs with his Purgatory Hill Harp, he put up a MySpace page under the name of Purgatory Hill. "I went to Johnny Lowebow's MySpace and friended him there." Lowe liked what he heard and wrote back. Far from being annoyed, John encouraged mAcdonald to use the name.

Initially, Purgatory Hill just functioned as pat's alter ego. "I created a fictitious back-story on this character.* I became Purgatory Hill and acquired all that fake mythology associated with that character."

Along the way, pat had started recording his Hill Harp-based songs. "I was making a disc. I thought originally I was going to call it *Reset* for the song 'Reset Me Lord.'" In three separate sessions he recorded everything he'd written on "that thing."

"Finally, [on] the third try, I recorded everything I knew on it and I had the feeling it was worthwhile, that I could whip it into an album, so I did that. That's what we have: the *Purgatory Hill* album."

"melaniejane's a big presence on that album—she plays hand percussion, sings backing vocals, and adds touches of keyboard. When we started doing shows as a duo, just doing the Purgatory Hill portion of the set, it made sense at that point to call our band, our duo, Purgatory Hill. Whatever we do as a duo is Purgatory Hill.

"When I started doing songs on the Hill Harp…whenever I took that thing out, that seemed like the most climactic part of our set, the part that seemed to engage the crowd most. So, like Pavlov's dog, I started playing it more and more."

Surprised though he may be at having taken up a "whole new instrument" at this stage of his career, mAcdonald no longer feels the need to play a "normal" guitar. John Lowe's assemblage of cigar box, dowels, hose clamps, inner tubes, and sewing machine bobbins—variously known as Purgatory Hill Harp, cigar box guitar and "That Thing"—seems perfectly suited to pat's playing style and to Purgatory Hill's signature sound.

"It is kinda cool; I've never really felt like part of any kind of scene or style or genre or movement in music. With this Cigar Box Nation or this whole homemade instruments movement…this is the first time I've really felt like part of any kind of group.

**Slide CBG.** pat wears his slide on his pinkie finger.

## MACDONALD NO LONGER FEELS THE NEED TO PLAY A "NORMAL" GUITAR.

"It's a strange group—a lot of different people coming from a lot of different places and they have that one thing in common, and that is that the instruments are homemade and heavily based on a container that cigars came in."

"It's kind of a funny way to start a movement, and yet, why not?" ∎

---

* My mother, Heaven Williams (aka Heaven Hill), rest her soul, was a distiller's daughter, and a tea-totaller all her life. She met my father, a rounder, a drifter, "a good client," in the burlesque house she managed in Memphis, TN. She gave me the name "Purgatory" because it was, she said, "the nearest thing to Heaven I could find" and handed down the surname "Hill" (her stripper name) because she "liked it." (More details of my life will become available as they're created).

# Build #3:
# SIX-STRING ELECTRIC GUITAR

For my third cigar box guitar project, I'm going to turn a cigar box into an unconventional-looking, six-string electric guitar. I'm a big fan of the Fender Telecaster, so this cigar box guitar will be my homage to that classic, enduring design.

"The biggest rush (and addiction) to me is watching people's faces when they see a cigar box guitar for the first time. It seems that people go through three distinct phases: the 'What the heck is that thing?' phase, the 'Oh, but I'll bet it sounds like c**p' phase, and, finally, when they hear some good solid licks played on it, the 'I'll be doggone!!' phase. I'll NEVER get tired of watching the realization set in for people when the CBG proves itself to be a real instrument capable of some fine music."

**—MIKE BINGHAM, CIGAR BOX NATION**

## TOOLS LIST:

**NECESSARY:**

* 36" (915mm) yardstick
* Small steel ruler
* Pencil/marking knife
* Marking awl
* Coping saw
* Square
* Utility knife
* Four-in-hand
* Razor blade
* Masking tape
* 1x2 (19 x 38mm) piece of ½" (13mm) MDF
* Drill bits, Including Forstner bits
* Screwdrivers
* Files
* Rasps
* Chisel and mallet
* Router and straight bit with ball bearing guide
* Heavy C-clamp
* Soldering iron and solder
* Paraffin wax
* Small trim saw

**HELPFUL:**

* Drill press
* Scroll saw
* Table saw

## PARTS LIST

* Wiring diagram
* Cigar box
* Electric guitar neck. You can find these used through guitar repair shops, but if you don't mind cosmetic "blemishes," you can get good prices on new necks. I got mine (maple fretboard on maple neck) on eBay for under $30.
* Scrap lumber to fill your chosen cigar box, preferably something dense, like maple or oak, but any solid wood will do—the heavier the better.
* Shim stock
* Tele-style neck pickup
* Tele-style bridge pickup with mounting screws and springs
* Three-position selector switch
* (6) Guitar tuners
* (6) Press-fit tuner bushings
* (6) String ferrules or, if you're on a tight budget, brass eyelets (I used the eyelets in this build) to fit string ball ends
* (2) 250K ohm three-terminal potentiometers (pots), one for volume and one for tone
* Tele-style control mounting plate
* String tree
* (2) Strap buttons
* Tele-style neck plate with mounting screws
* Tele-style bridge
* Pick guard material (I used scraps from a broken guard)
* .047 capacitor

# PART I:
# PREPARING AND ASSEMBLING MATERIALS

I found a fretted electric guitar neck on eBay—it's a gorgeous maple neck with a maple fret board. I got it at a good price because of a minor cosmetic issue. Once you've adopted the cigar box ethic, it gets really easy to overlook cosmetic issues.

I ordered pickups, electronic parts, and hardware new from an online retailer for expediency's sake, but given the enormous number of guitars purchased, broken, upgraded, retired, and resold on any given day, acquiring the requisite parts used or salvaged shouldn't be a major challenge. My total tab for parts was about $150. If I'd taken a bit more time to source parts, I'm certain I could have found everything I needed for less money by visiting resale shops, guitar stores, repair centers, and just generally asking around. These aren't authentic Fender parts, but are inexpensive copies. For me, it's part of the cigar box guitar ethic to spend as little as possible on my builds, even if I'm trying to build a six-string electric. Bill Jehle once challenged himself to build an electric six-string guitar for as little money as possible and accomplished his goal for under $10. He performs with his.

If you unsure of where to look for guitar parts, try some of these online retailers:

◆ C.B. Gitty

◆ Stewart Macdonald

◆ Guitar Fetish

◆ War Moth

◆ eBay

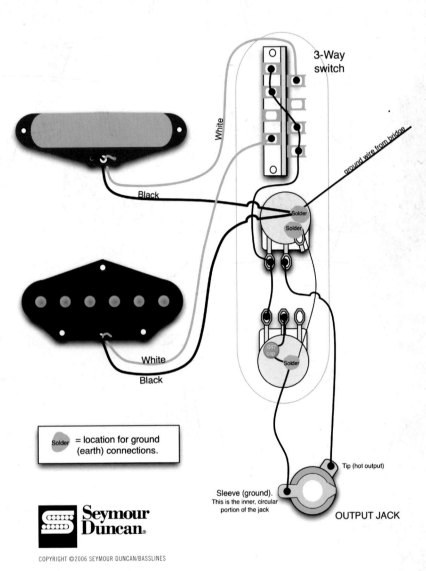

**Wiring diagram.** I downloaded mine from Seymour Duncan's Web site (http://www.seymourduncan.com/support/wiring-diagrams). There are a number of different ways to wire a Telecaster-style guitar with two pickups and a three-way switch. I've chosen the standard wiring setup.

**The winner.** I've settled on this long, black box for the body of my six-string electric guitar. The red one's nearly identical, so I'll use that box to work out some of the construction details and for practice.

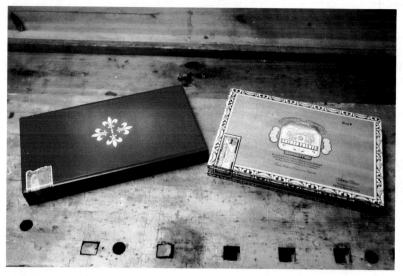

**Cigar box.** The longer the better. I have chosen from a number of oversized cigar boxes. The natural color box on the right looked good but wasn't deep enough to support the neck. It's not essential that the box be as long as the one I chose. As long as the brige/tailpiece assembly fits on the box, you're good to go. Measure your neck scale, lay the bridge in place, and see if your box will support it.

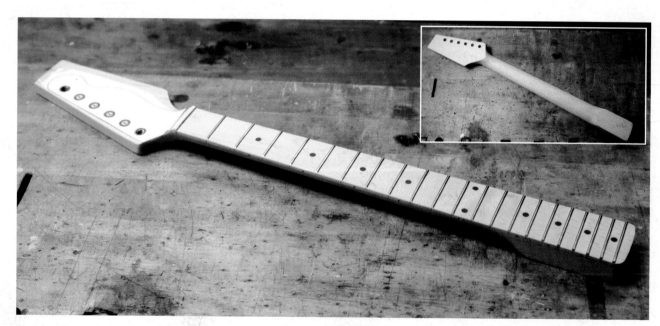

**Electric guitar neck.** Building a six-string guitar neck with an adjustable truss rod is beyond the scope of this project. Guitar necks are available from many different sources; I found this beautiful maple neck with a maple fretboard on eBay priced at about $30 due to minor cosmetic flaws.

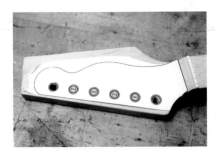

**Headstock template.** A quick Internet search produced a Telecaster headstock outline that I sized to fit and glued in place.

**Lumber.** I'm going to stuff the inside of my cigar box with wood so that it's nearly solid. By measuring the inside of the bottom and the top, I've determined that I'll need roughly 1¼" (32mm) of wood to fill the box from bottom to top. I have some ¾" (19mm)-thick maple and some ½" (13mm) poplar on hand that will work.

**Shim stock.** I said *roughly* 1¼" (32mm). I'll need a layer or two of veneer-thickness wood to add to the the other lumber to fill the box just to the top. I picked this "veneer" up at the cigar store; it's actually cigar packaging.

**Electronics and hardware.** Clockwise from upper left: Tele-style neck pickup; Tele-style bridge pickup with mounting screws and springs; three-position selector switch; six guitar tuners; press-fit tuner bushings; two 250K ohm three-terminal potentiometers (pots), one for volume and one for tone.

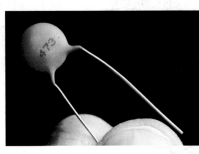

**Capacitor.**

**Tele-style bridge.**

**Tele-style control mounting plate.**

**Volume/Tone pots.**

Three-position selector switch with knob.

Bridge pickup.

Neck pickup.

String tree.

Strap buttons.

Tele-style neck plate with mounting screws.

Tele-style volume/tone knobs.

**Broken pick guard.** I'll take a slice out of this old bass guitar pick guard to fashion a pick guard for my guitar.

# PART II:
# BUILDING

This build assumes you can operate a soldering iron and read a simple wiring diagram. I'll offer some of what I've learned about soldering, but detailed instruction is beyond our scope here. Once again, there are many fine Internet sites that can help, and the two major cigar box guitar social networks, *www.cigarboxnation.com* and *handmademusicclubhouse.com*, have much to offer on the subject.

I borrowed a Tele from my friend, singer/songwriter Al Day, to get a feel for it and to transfer some important measurements. I recommend that you get your hands on a guitar too, or at least visit a music store or get some pictures for reference on the Internet. In the following steps, I will tell you what measurements I got from my reference, but keep in mind that your reference may be different.

**Al's Telecaster.** This is the real-life Fender Telecaster my friend—the brilliant singer/songwriter Al Day—graciously loaned me for inspiration and guidance.

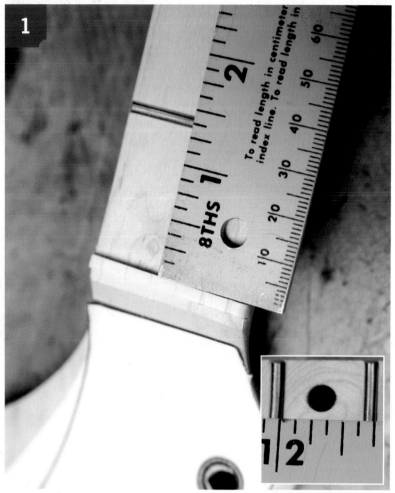

**Remember scale length.** Jot the scale length down in an easy-to-find location.

**Determine scale length.** To begin, determine the scale length of the fretted neck. To do this, place the end of a yard stick against the nut, then take a reading at the twelfth fret. Nut to twelfth fret is half the total scale length. My twelfth fret is just a millimeter short of 12¾" (324mm), giving me a scale length of 25½" (648mm). I'll need to center the adjustable bridge at 25½" (648mm) from the nut.

**Headstock: Get inspiration.** I'm using my borrowed Telecaster as a guide. I suggest you borrow one too, or at least find some photos on the Internet or visit a guitar at your local music store.

**Headstock: Cut the shape.** Use repositionable spray adhesive to attach the template to the headstock. Rough out the headstock shape with a scroll saw. A coping saw works well, too.

**Headstock: Finish the shape.** Refine the shape and clean up the edges with your four-in-hand.

**Headstock: Cleaning off the pattern.** Remove the pattern. Use a razor as a scraper to remove all the residual glue. Even if you can't see it, glue residue can interfere with finish absorption, so clean carefully.

**Headstock: Pretty good!** I think my headstock comes pretty close to the original. I'll take that sharp corner off at the bottom left with my four-in-hand and call it good.

**Transfer measurements.** First, cover the box with painter's masking tape in order to protect the finish and to give you something to write and draw on as you go. Then, use your reference guitar to determine the location of the neck pocket, neck pickup, and approximate location of the bridge and bridge pickup. Also locate the center line of the box/guitar body. Note that I perform these marking and cutting steps on my practice cigar box first, before working on my "keeper" box. If you aren't doing a practice box first, that's OK too. Just be careful. Mark the control panel position on the lid. I eyeballed it; centered between the strings and the side of the box. I used Al's telecaster as a guide for north and south vis a vis the metal bridge plate.

**Measurements: Neck seating above.** My guitar's neck has the same thickness as Al's Telecaster's neck. I need to know how much of the neck remains above the body: ⁷⁄₁₀" (18mm). Transfer this mark to your guitar neck.

**Measurements: Neck seating below.** I also need to know how much of the neck sits into down into the body: 2⅖" (61mm).

**Measurements: Neck center.** Locate the center line of the neck and mark it with a marker.

**Neck pocket: Make a pattern.** Cut a piece of MDF to the same size as the cigar box, and use that to create a pattern for the router to follow.

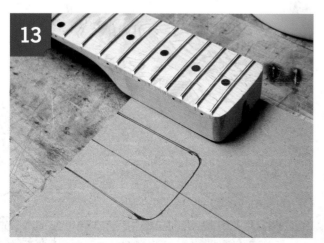

**Neck pocket: Transfer the neck shape.** Trace the neck heel's profile on the MDF.

**Neck pocket: Cut the pattern.** Go back to the scroll saw to cut out the pattern.

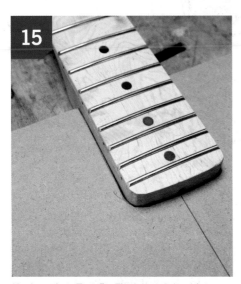

**15**

Neck pocket: **Test fit.** Fit the neck heel into the pattern and touch it up with files where necessary. You want the neck to fit cleanly into the pocket, but not too tightly. Hold on to the pattern; you won't actually cut the neck pocket until Step 46.

**16**

**Remove the box lid.** This is optional, but generally a good idea. It just makes maneuvering that much simpler. This particular lid is attached with a staple-like hinge. The prongs are set into the wood and then bent over. BE SURE TO UN-BEND the pointy part as much as possible before you try to pull the hinge out, or you could end up breaking that delicate piece of wood. I'm suggesting you do it here even though I tried for a while working with the lid still in place. I DON'T recommend you work with the lid in place any longer than you need to; it just complicates things.

**17**

**Filling: Select ¾" (20mm) fill pieces.** Select a piece of 1x6 (19 x 140mm) and 1x3 (19 x 63mm) to fill in the cigar box. I like maple because it's dense and heavy, which makes for good tone, but use whatever wood you like.

**18**

**Filling: Cut the 1x6 (19 x 140mm).** Cut the 1x6 (19 x 140mm) to length for a snug fit. Remember, if you try to force a slightly oversized piece of wood into the box...the box will lose that contest.

**Filling: Cut the 1x3 (19 x 63mm).** Rip the 1x3 (19 x 63mm) to width with a table saw or hand saw. This will take up the remaining width at the top of the box. Cut it to length so as to leave a chamber for the controls (the gap below the 1x3). Make sure it is long enough to support the screw that will hold the top end of the control panel plate in place.

**Filling: Cut the ½" (13mm) piece.** Now, move to the ½" (13mm) poplar and cut a piece long enough to fill the top of the box from side to side, and just wide enough to leave room for the neck pickup. My neck pickup was ½" (13mm) from the heel of the neck; I took that measurement from the Tele.

**Neck pickup: Reinforce the lid.** In preparation for cutting a pickup opening in the box lid, cut a piece of scrap to fit inside the lid. The scrap should be at least as wide as the pickup, and should fit the whole way across the lid. The wood used in most cigar boxes is thin and soft. Without the backing piece to drill into and against, the inside of the lid would splinter. If the drill you use is on the heavy side, it could even pop through and leave a hole in the back of the box.

**Neck pickup: Select a Forstner bit.** Select a bit slightly smaller than the neck pickup. While a Forstner isn't required here, I'm choosing one for two reasons: it will pull through the work more slowly than a twist bit would; and it will give me cleaner edges than a twist bit.

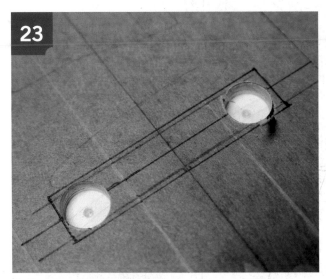

**23**

**Neck pickup: Drill the holes.** Because I'll have a pick guard over this cutout, my hole doesn't need to be a perfect fit, but I'm taking this opportunity to practice cutting the shape to fit the pickup—as I'll do when I make the pick guard. Drill one hole on each end of the rectangle you marked out.

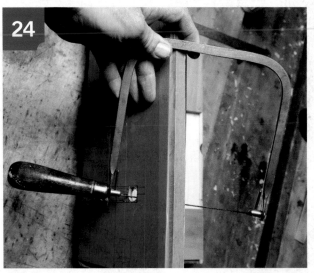

**24**

**Neck pickup: Set up the coping saw.** Detach the blade from your coping saw, thread it through the opening, and reconnect it.

**25**

**Neck pickup: Finish cutting the opening.** Use the coping saw to connect the two holes. You may want to clamp the lid—GENTLY—to help keep things still while you saw.

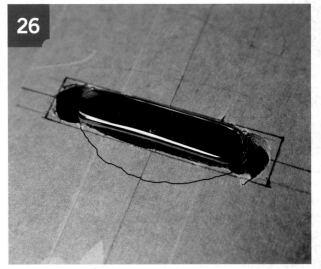

**26**

**Neck pickup: Check the fit.** With the pickup in place in the box, I replaced the box lid to check the fit. Remove the semi-circular area indicated so the pickup can be removed, if necessary, without taking the top off the box. Make sure the semicircle fits your particular pickup.

**Neck pickup: Test fit mounting screws.** Maple is very hard. It's easy to snap off a screw if you try to force it into this wood. Drill two different sized holes in a test piece of maple to determine which bit to use for the screws to mount the neck pickup. The threads have a firm grip, but the screw must turn easily, without excessive force. Near the screw, you can see bits of the paraffin I use to lubricate the screw threads to ease their path.

**Neck pickup: Situate the mounting screws.** Install the two mounting screws so the neck pickup will be right next to the ½" (13mm) poplar piece. Put the pickup aside for now.

**Bridge: Get the plate ready.** Locate and mark the center line of the bridge plate so it is easy to center it on the box.

**Bridge: Center and square.** Make sure the bridge is dead center and the correct distance from the guitar's nut—the functional bridge should be at 25½" (648mm). Use a square to ensure the plate is square to the edges of the box. Next, trace its shape, the opening, and the screw hole positions onto the box.

**31**

**Bridge: Mark the opening for the pickup.** Using the bridge outline as a guide to position the bridge pickup, outline the bridge pickup so you can create an opening to fit.

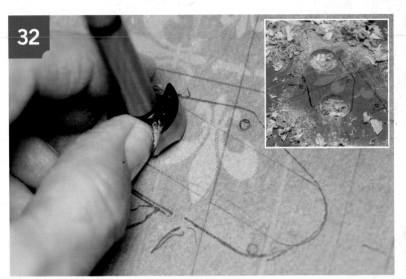

**32**

**Bridge: Drill, cut, and file.** Once again, use a Fostner bit to start the opening. Select a bit that will occupy the same general area on your guitar as shown in this photo. Follow the same procedure as before, drilling holes, then using a coping saw, and finally using rasps and/or files to finish the opening to size.

**33**

**Bridge: Finish off the pickup hole.** Be sure to fit a backing board behind the opening to support the wood and prevent tearout. Rotate the lid and move the backing board as you make your way around the cut-out to prevent spintering and tearout all the way around.

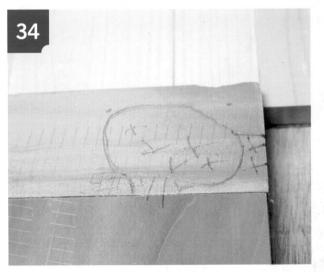

**34**

**Filling: Finish filling the box.** Select several more pieces of ½" (13mm) poplar to fill the area over the 1x6 and below the neck pickup. Be sure to mark the area to create a cutaway to house the bridge pickup.

**35**

**Filling: Cut the bridge pickup recess.** It was simpler to cut this piece with a coping saw before gluing it into place.

**36**

**Filling.** Cut the last piece of ½" (13mm) poplar to fill in the rest of the space. Remember to leave a cavity for the neck pickup. After making sure the lid fits properly, glue this last round of fill pieces in place.

**37**

**Filling: Make a wire channel.** Chisel out a channel to get the neck pickup wires down to the control panel.

**38**

**Jack: Select a drill bit.** The output jack will be the last piece of hardware you need to make a home for. Use a drill bit sizer or ruler to help select the appropriate size drill bit for this opening.

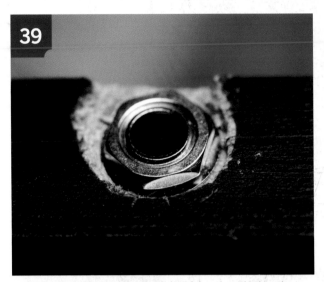

**Jack: Countersink.** If the box wall is thicker than the length of the jack's mounting shaft (which is likely given that the most common jacks were designed to be mounted through a pickguard) you'll need to counterbore slightly to allow the washer and nut to seat. Best to counterbore before you drill the working hole. If you don't have a countersink bit, use a larger Forstner bit. Drill all the holes needed for the jack, and remember to reinforce the box wall with scrap wood while you drill.

**Jack: Test fit.** The output jack fits securely in place, but you'll want to reinforce the box wall at this spot, too. Remember, cigar boxes are built from from thin, soft woods. They're shipping boxes; not built to last. Putting a large hole through the wall will weaken it, and this is a stress point. You'll be plugging and unplugging for years to come.

**Jack: Cut reinforcement to fit.** Cut a small piece of ½" (13mm) poplar to reinforce the corner of the box. Put it in place temporarily and mark the center point of the hole drilled in the box wall so you can center your drill bit later.

**Jack: Select a drill bit.** Find a Forstner or spade bit just larger than the entire output jack.

**Jack: Drill the reinforcement.** I cut the hole to center around the smaller jack mounting hole.

**Jack: Test fit the reinforcement.** Make sure it all fits together; then remove the reinforcement.

**Jack: Add more wood!** The second reason wood is needed down here is that you'll need something to drive the bottom control panel mounting screw into. So, cut another piece of poplar similar to the first. Put the pieces in place and sit the control panel on it to make sure there is enough wood. Add more as needed; then glue and clamp it all together.

**Neck pocket: Prepare to cut.** Carefully center the neck pocket jig onto the cigar box. Use two small pieces of double-sided carpet tape to hold it in place, as well as some clamps. The clamps will do a pretty good job, but the tape offers an extra margin of security. When I did a test run of this operation, the router knocked the end piece of the box lid out of place, so I modified my approach a bit, using a small trim saw to cut that delicate piece by hand on both sides before routing.

**47**

**Neck pocket: Ready, go!** Set the router bit at about a third of the final depth. I used a ½" (13mm) bit. Working CLOCKWISE (against the bit's rotation), make your way around the pocket in several passes, increasing the depth with each pass.

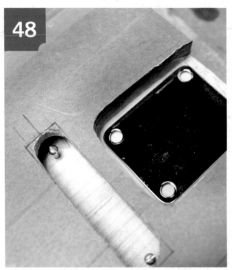

**48**

**Neck pocket: Mark the bolt mounting holes.** I use the neck mounting plate to position drill holes for the neck mounting bolts.

**49**

**Neck pocket: Drill straight holes.** Move to the drill press for this operation. These bolts are critical to having a straight guitar neck, so the holes must be straight and true. They must also be drilled large enough to allow the screws to pass through without gripping. If you want to draw two pieces of wood together with a screw, the screw cannot grip in the piece closer to the head of the screw. If the threads grip both pieces, the two boards will remain equidistant apart and not draw together. In a sense, the board closer to the screw head is sandwiched between two things: The head of the screw and the board that the threads are actually gripping. The piece between needs to float.

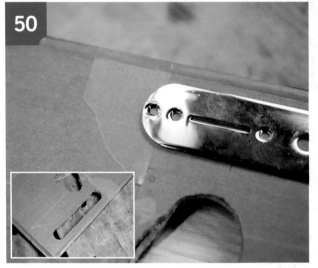

**50**

**Control panel: Mark placement.** To help with placing the screw hole, use a smaller piece of tape to indicate where the wood begins underneath the lid. When the panel is in place and straight, trace its outline onto the box, then drill and cut as you did for the other openings.

**Control panel: Finish the opening.** Be conservative cutting this opening—you can always expand it, but you want to make sure the control panel covers the entire opening.

**Pick guard: Make the first cuts.** I'm using a scavenged pick guard to create one for my guitar. If you're doing the same, cut a slice out of the old guard and put it on the guitar body to get a feel for it.

**Pick guard: Refine the shape.** I happened to like one of the existing curves, so I traced that curve and recreated it on the opposite side, making a symmetrical shape. Do whatever takes your fancy.

**Pick guard: Make the pickup opening.** Employing the same technique used for the opening in the box top (Steps 23–26), start by cutting two holes in the guard, then cut the center out with a coping saw.

**55**

Pick guard: **Refine the opening.** Finish the opening with a rasp and file. This material is thin and brittle, so be sure to back it up (as I have here with a vise).

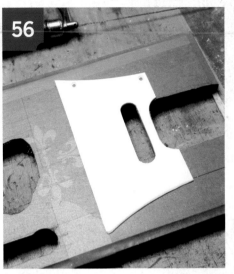

**56**

Pick guard: **Test fit.** Put the pick guard in place and make sure to drill and countersink any screw holes that are needed.

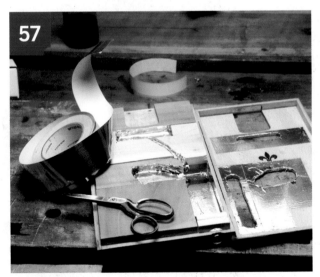

**57**

**Add shielding.** The pros line the component cavity with carefully fitted copper sheeting, folded and soldered together, to provide shielding from ambient electromagnetic radiation (think fluorescent lights) that can cause electric guitars to buzz. I recommend a roll of aluminum metal furnace tape to line the compartment. This won't offer quite the protection that the professional job would, but it's a simple solution that will offer a modicum of protection.

**58**

**Bridge: Double check the bridge position.** Now is a good time to make sure the bridge location line is right where it should be.

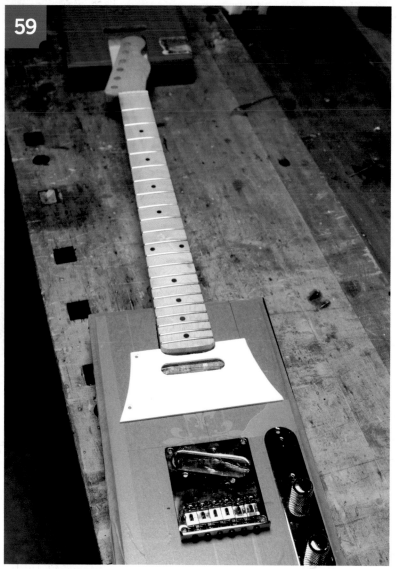

**59**

**Impatient man's preview.** Now is also the perfect time to get a preview of what the cigar box "Telecaster" will look like; put the hardware on the box with the neck in place. I'll admit it. I'm getting excited.

**60**

**Tuners: Install the bushings.** We'll install two guitar strings to act as plumb lines for the final neck alignment. You've already placed the holes for the neck mounting screws very carefully. In order to attach strings, you must attach the tuners. Start by installing the press-fit tuner bushings.

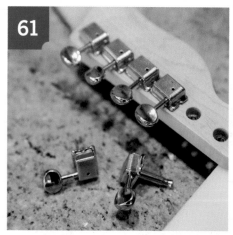

**61**

**Tuners: Position the tuners.** With the bushings in place, carefully line up the tuners in position. Use a straightedge to align the housings.

**Tuners: Drill holes for tuner screws.** My headstock here is just ½" (13mm) thick (yours is probably thin too) and I don't want to drill all the way through. Set the drill to a slow speed setting and affix a masking tape depth guide to the bit. Be sure the pilot holes are large enough and deep enough to accommodate the screws, or you could snap them off in the wood.

**62**

**Tuners: Install.** Drive in the screws to secure the tuners.

**Bridge: Attach the bridge.** Position the bridge and attach it with just the bottom two screws to support the strings you'll use as plumb lines later.

**Neck: Prepare clamping pads.** In the next few steps, I recommend using a heavy iron C-clamp to hold the neck in place while you plumb it to the guitar body. Here's a tip I read about years ago: Use a Forstner bit to drill shallow holes in scraps of wood, just deep enough to hold a pair of round magnets. Superglue the magnets in place. These clamping pads will be easy to keep in place and align.

**Neck: Position the neck for mounting.** I have Bill Jehle to thank for walking me through this process. First, secure the bottom end of the guitar in a face vise so the guitar stands vertically, then clamp the neck in place in its pocket.

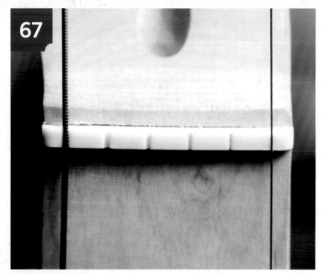

**Neck: Install test strings.** Install the two E strings as plumb lines.

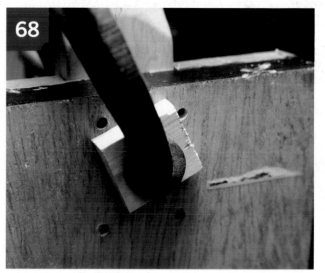

**Neck: Check mounting holes.** Make sure the mounting screw holes remain accessible.

**Neck: Plumb the neck.** With the clamp snug and the guitar body stable, move the neck side-to-side in its pocket until the strings align with the neck.

**Neck: Mark the hole positions.** Use a drill bit to mark the heel of the neck for the mounting screws.

**71**

**Neck: Measure screw depth.** Establish how much of the screw will actually penetrate the neck.

**72**

**Neck: Drill holes.** Go to the drill press once again to assure straight pilot holes. Use masking tape to mark the drill bit the same depth as the screw you measured in the last step. Because the fret board has a radius, the neck itself must be cradled to prevent it from rocking and to prevent damage to the frets.

**73**

**Neck: Test fit.** This is a test install. With the neck screwed fast and the strings in place, make sure everything lines up as it should. There's more work to do with the body, so detach the neck and set it aside for now to keep it safe and make the body more manageable.

**74**

**Bridge: Drill string ports.** This bridge is designed so the strings install from the back of the guitar. Using the bridge as a guide, use the drill press to drill string ports all the way through the body of the guitar.

**75**

**Bridge: Reinforce the string ports.** Use brass eyelets (rivets) to reinforce the openings of the string ports. This will keep the string ball ends from being pulled deeper into the wood. Counterbore the string holes at ¾₆" (5mm) on the back. Epoxy the rivets in place. *After using this guitar for a while, I opted to replace these brass rivets with Fender-style string cups. Take your pick. The cups cost a few bucks, but they hold the ball-end of the string below the surface so they're out of the way; you never feel them against your body.

**76**

**Neck pickup: Install.** Using the two screws already in place, install the neck pickup and support springs. The screws go in just far enough to support the pickup—make the final height adjustment in the setup process. CAUTION: Handle your pickups with extreme care. The copper wire used to wind guitar pickups is finer than a human hair. It's hard to see, hard to work with, and extremely easy to break. The insulated wire leads coming off the pickup connect to these ultra-fine copper wires right where they meet the pickup mounting plate.

**77**

**Control panel: Finalize the cutout.** If necessary, widen the control panel cutout just a bit to allow the pots to slide in and out without removing the entire box top.

**78**

**Control panel: Attach pots to mounting plate.** Attaching the pots to the mounting plate with their retaining nuts makes them easier to manage during wiring.

**79**

**Bridge: Test fit bridge and bridge pickup.** Test fit the bridge and bridge pickup, and adjust the internal opening as needed.

**80**

**Wiring: Solder prep.** One of the most difficult soldering processes for me to get was getting solder to stick to the back of a pot. All the soldering tips come into play here, but the most helpful suggestion I got for pots was to clean the back with paint thinner or acetone to remove oil or other residue and to rough the surface slightly with fine emery cloth or sandpaper. Heat the back of the pot with your soldering iron and run a few drops of solder to stick to the back of the pot. You'll know it's really on if it spreads on the flat surface. If it balls up, it's not really stuck and you need to reheat the back of the pot until the solder flows out.

## MAGNETIC PARTS KEEPER

I keep an assortment of magnets of various shapes and sizes in my shop because I find them useful in all sorts of ways. Here, a stack of round magnets act as a a parts corral for crucial pickup mounting springs and screws that are easy to lose and hard to replace.

**Wiring: Follow the diagram.** Carefully following the wiring diagram you've chosen, cleanly solder all connections. Check and double check all connections, polarities, and solder joints. I recommend doing all the wiring outside of the box. You can actually test the connections at this stage by plugging your wiring harness into an amplifier and tapping on the pickup with a metal screwdriver.

**Wiring: Install the bridge pickup.** Mount the bridge pickup in the bridge.

**Wiring: Drill hole for ground wire.** The electronics need to be grounded to the bridge, so drill a hole under the bridge to feed the ground wire through.

**Wiring: Put everything else in place.** Get all the electronic parts in place, including the control plate, bridge, and pickups.

**85**

**Pick guard: Mark the box for the pick guard.** Position the pick guard over the neck pickup. Mark the box for screw holes, then drill pilot holes for the screws. Screw the pick guard in place.

**86**

**Neck: Attach the neck.** Attach the neck and neck mounting plate.

**87**

**Final touches: Secure the box lid.** Fix the box lid in place with several screws, dressing them up with decorative brass washers.

**88**

**Final touches: Position the strap buttons.** Drill holes for mounting the top and bottom strap button. I center one button at the tail end of the guitar and position the other on the "top."

**Final touches: Attach the strap buttons.** Screw in the strap buttons.

**Final touches: Mount the string tree.** Use a marking awl to position the string tree, which holds the longest strings tightly against the nut (increases string break) for optimum vibration and tone.

**Final touches: String it up!** Add all the strings to the guitar.

**Test run.** This is the thrilling climax where you finally get to plug in your axe and start making some noise! In my case, however, it was a thrilling anti-climax and time to call in some help. No sound! If this happens to you too, check out the following section on troubleshooting.

# PART III:

# TROUBLESHOOTING

As this was my first attempt at building and wiring an electric guitar, I planned to see my friend, Terry Straker (owner of the world-famous Guitar Works in Evanston, Illinois), when I finished.

In the end, my finished guitar required some electronic troubleshooting, and Terry was able to quickly isolate and solve the problems for me—which was an education in itself—before we went on to setup.

Guitar Works in Evanston has done business with and made repairs for The Who, John Fogerty, Los Lobos, Smashing Pumpkins, The Ramones, Chet Atkins, Johnny Winter, and dozens of other musicians whose music you've enjoyed. What better place to stop by and pick up a few pointers?

Terry started off with a visual inspection of my wiring job, which immediately turned up a mistake. He was able to address that by moving a wire to where it should have been.

We still couldn't get any sound out, so Straker turned to testing circuits. To accomplish this, Terry brought out his multi-tester—an inexpensive (under $15) electronic tool—that he uses to check electrical circuits. After discovering more than one possible problem, Terry opted to clip all the wires free from the three-position switch and simply start over—the clean slate approach—an approach I also recommend when you're confronted with multiple possible errors.

He found two more minor problems. In one case, a tiny wire strand, barely visible to the naked eye, had created a short. When he'd remedied that, the bridge pickup worked, but the neck pickup did not. A high-magnification inspection of the neck pickup's lead wires revealed that the micro-fine copper winding wire had broken away from the lead wire. With the deft hands of an expert safecracker, Straker unwrapped the winding, found the end of the hair-fine winding wire, and re-soldered it to the lead.

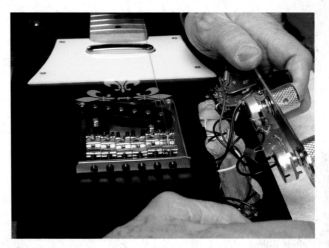

**Inspection.** Terry does a visual inspection of my wiring job. You should do the same to your guitar.

**Fixing wire placement.** Here, Terry is fixing a misplaced wire in my guitar. Compare your wiring diagram to what you actually produced. If no sound is coming out, it may be that you have soldered a wire to the wrong place.

**Checking circuits.** Another potential issue is an incomplete or shorted circuit. Make sure to check those, too.

# PART IV:
# SETUP

Terry also went over guitar setup with me. Setup is the final tune-up and adjustment all guitars should get as a last step before playing. First off, Straker checked the neck for straightness. The neck checked out fine, so he gave the frets a close visual inspection and also ran a small steel rule lengthwise along the neck. The rule kept catching on the eleventh fret, indicating that that fret was higher than the rest. After first marking the tops of frets 10, 11, and 12 with ink, Straker went to work with a flat file to bring the high fret back in line. When the ink started to rub off the two frets adjacent to the eleventh, he knew he'd reached the correct height.

After filing the frets, Straker reached for his fret-crowning file. The eleventh fret in particular had become quite flat, and it was up to the crowning file to return the frets to their domed shape. He crowned each fret carefully, keeping a close watch on the file marks from his leveling efforts. He wanted to make sure his crowning would leave just a trace of those marks—a way of ensuring he didn't lower the frets any farther.

The neck I used has a fretboard with a radius, giving it a very slight arc. Terry reached for a set of radius gauges to determine that the radius of the arc was 14" (355mm).

**Evening out frets.** If you have a high fret, be sure to file it down until it is level with all the others.

**Crowning frets.** If you need to file down frets, be sure to restore their crowned shape afterward.

**Measuring radius.** If you have a radius gauge, make sure your strings are at the proper placement for the fretboard's radius.

**Correcting string action.** If you find that your strings are too high to play comfortably, use gauged nut files to carefully remove mass from the nut string groove. Go slowly, a little at a time, and check as you go!

**Adjusting string length.** Use a screwdriver to fine-tune the length of each string.

**Confirming string length.** Here, Terry is using a virtual strobe tuner to verify the string length. You could also use an electric tuner; see text.

**Tuning the strings.** The final step is tuning the strings. Then, start playing!

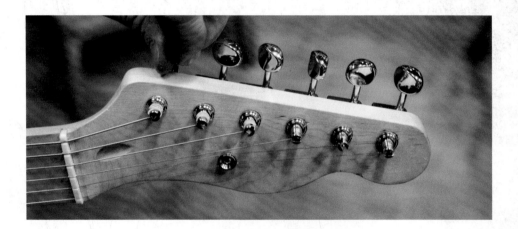

Using the height adjustment screws in the bridge, he set the string heights to conform to that same 14" (355mm) radius.

Next, Straker turned his attention to the string action, or the height of each string over the frets. The strings need to be low enough so they're playable, but if they're too low, they'll buzz against the frets when played. The right string height or action depends on the player's style, comfort, and hand strength—it's highly individualized. This is a slow process—using gauged nut files, he removed just a little of the nut at a time and rechecked the string height frequently. If you go too far too fast with this step, there's no recourse other than to create a new nut, and that's pretty involved.

The final step in this setup process will be to adjust each string's intonation. Each individual string, fretted at the twelfth fret, should sound a perfect octave above the pitch it sounds open (unfretted).

This bridge has fine adjustment screws that Terry moves forward or back, making tiny changes in each string's overall length until each sounds a perfect octave at the twelfth fret.

Terry plugs the guitar into his virtual strobe tuner (for our purposes, a good ear or an inexpensive electronic guitar tuner, available for $10-$12, will do). Using a Phillips head screwdriver, Terry moves each string support in the bridge until the pitch of the open string reads one full octave below the pitch of the string fretted at the twelfth fret.

If the string sounds sharper fretted than it does open, the half of the string that's sounding—bottom half—is shorter than the top half. In this case, we'd want to lengthen it by moving the adjustable bridge *away* from the headstock until the string produces the same note/pitch whether the string is plucked open or fretted at the twelfth.

All that's left is to tune it up and play!

# GALLERY: SIX-STRING CBGS

Take a gander at these six-string beauties. Each CBG in this gallery has a plethora
of strings, and a different way of placing them. Most are also electric.

**Dolorosa, headstock.** Headstock; maple neck with
rosewood fingerboard.

**Dolorosa, artwork.** Close-up of silk-screened sacred
heart artwork.

**Daddy Mojo, six-string "Dolorosa" model.** Six-string electric with violin style f-holes and
mini-humbucker style pickup.

**Steampunk Elizabeth, headstock.** Denman decorated the headstock with a heart-shaped locket and a button from a pair of jeans.

**Steampunk Elizabeth, detail.** Denman pulled gears from an old pocket watch and a radio-controlled car to help punk Elizabeth out.

**Steampunk Elizabeth, bottom details.** Other components include: compass, ½" (13mm) copper pipe, automobile taillight bulbs, compass body, and three F-holes trimmed with gold paint.

**Steampunk Elizabeth six-string electric by Shawn Denman.** Denman started with the neck from a First Act Strat copy he found at the Salvation Army to build this six-string electric. He fastened two "Tabak Coffee Infused Cigar" boxes together for the body. He also pulled both pickups, accompanying electronics, and the bridge from the First Act. What looks like a railroad spike on the right is actually half of a chrome shoe-horn. Denman affixed the other half of the shoe horn to the copper pipe visible at left.

**Tomi-O six-string, headstock.** The straight-forward headstock is rugged and built for strength.

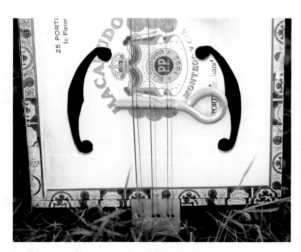

**Tomi-O six-string, soundholes.** Tomi-O used paired strings on this build for a fuller sound.

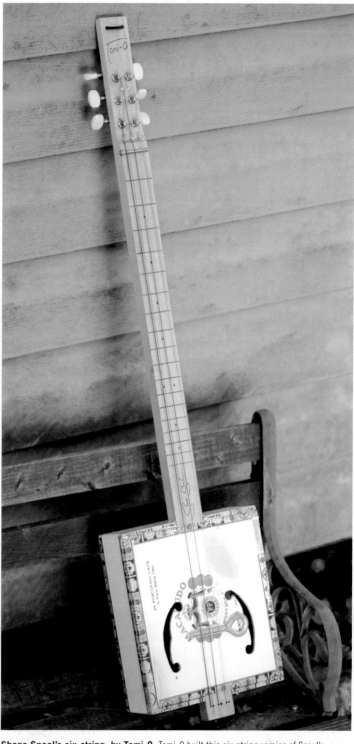

**Shane Speal's six-string, by Tomi-O.** Tomi-O built this six-string version of Speal's "Old Faithful" (page 35).

**Smokehouse Cohiba six-string electric.** Built by Josh Gayou of Smokehouse Guitars in southern California.

**Smokehouse Cohiba, headstock.** The assymetrical tuner layout makes for an attractive headstock.

**Smokehouse Cohiba, saddle and pickup.** Handsome rosewood detailing.

**Smokehouse Cohiba, knobs.** "Boost" and "Frequency Expansion" switches and the volume control knob.

# MIKE ORR
## HARRISBURG, PENNSYLVANIA

*I spoke with Mike Orr by phone in February 2011. Mike's an enthusiastic builder and concert-goer, and though I had not met him in person, I did have the pleasure of seeing a number of his guitars at the York, PA, festival. Among them I saw the peculiar, yet acoustically viable, "shitar," which utilizes a metal bedpan as a resonating chamber. Check out Mike's book, Handmade Music Factory, for information on building other instruments from scratch.*

In 2005, Mike Orr was trolling eBay for a four-string tenor guitar. "I just thought it would be easier to play," he said. He didn't find the tenor guitar he was looking for, but he did find—quite unexpectedly—a way to support his passion for attending music festivals during the summers.

While searching for the four-string guitar, Orr discovered the newly formed Yahoo Cigar Box Guitar group. "It was just a small Yahoo group . . . I was the 18th member." Instead of buying a tenor guitar, Orr tapped into the resources available through the Yahoo group and eventually built one himself with a cigar box: "That's what got me started on the whole thing." His flooring business had been a little slow since the economic downturn, so he had some time to fill. For six months or so, Orr built cigar box guitars in his spare time, primarily for his own amusement, and gave them away to friends and family.

Orr's passion for attending music festivals during the summer isn't cheap. He soon hit on the idea of building cigar box guitars to sell at the festivals: "That's what got me into doing the vending, building them to sell. If you're not vending anything and you're just going out there, traveling two states away to camp out for the weekend and see some musical groups, it gets quite expensive. We tried [selling] tie-dyed T-shirts and different things like that. A friend of mine pointed out to me that the guitars would be something at the festivals that would be different, that no one else has, and boy was he right. It's been really great going out to the music festivals, renting a booth, and setting up—you get a better camping spot and [the trip] ends up paying for itself." Orr said he does well his with cigar box guitars at music festivals, selling 15–20 on a good weekend. Concentrating on the eastern seaboard, he's sold cigar box guitars from Florida up to Maine.

**Mike Orr.** Mike relaxes with one of his creations at a music festival.

At times, however, his musical tastes and the market for his guitars don't quite mesh. "I'm into the Grateful Dead scene, but those kids got no money and they'd much rather waste their money on booze. But when I do the artsy stuff for the bluegrass festivals, that's where the market's really at."

As of this writing, Orr had sold close to six hundred cigar box guitars at festivals and through eBay. As cigar box guitars have gained in popularity over the past few years, Orr has noticed the landscape changing a bit. "It's getting big ever since they put out that PBS documentary, [Max Shores'] *Songs Inside the Box*." Orr said he can tell where the documentary has been broadcast by watching for regional spikes in his eBay sales.

In an effort to stay on the crest of the wave, Orr has moved from just selling guitars to selling his own pre-made necks, fretboards, and wiring systems for people who want to build but who aren't quite ready to test their fretting or wiring skills. "I find that the people lately have been buying the fretboards with the frets already in them—they can just glue 'em on and go."

In addition to supplying parts to builders, Orr has expanded his festival offerings to include some more off-the-wall musical creations.

**Creating on the go.** Mike sometimes makes CBGs at the events he attends, which always draws a crowd.

PHOTO COURTESY JENNIFER STATLER PHOTOGRAPHY

"At first, I was sticking to the cigar boxes, and I was totally happy with it, but then every time I looked on eBay there was another guy selling 'em, and I thought I better widen my horizons and start building out of more than just cigar boxes. I think that's what got me the *Handmade Music Factory* [Fox Chapel Publishing, 2011] book deal."

"I built a cookie-tin three-string, a bedpan four-string slide guitar, a cigar box ukulele." Orr also built a six-string lap steel guitar onto an ironing board base. "A friend of mine plays lap and he wants to be able to set it up on the stage because he plays guitar too. He said it would be nice for him because he said he could just put his guitar down to the side and not even it take it off."

A bedpan? "I saw somebody playing one on YouTube or something, I think; they had a bedpan that they had just somehow bolted a six-string guitar neck onto." Orr built a four-string electric bedpan guitar using an antique enameled bedpan and a neck of his own making. He calls his creation a "shitar."

In addition to variations on the guitar theme, Orr has lately been converting old cassette decks he finds at flea markets into portable AC/DC guitar amplifiers. "Those little amps that I've been doin', I think they're gonna sell good."

Mike Orr's bad luck in finding a tenor guitar—a guitar that would be easy to play—led him down an unexpected path that he continues to enjoy even as he marvels at it. "The thing that really surprised me is the amount of people that have really got interested in it in the last few years; just how big it has gotten. That group of Shane [Speal]'s, the one that was just 18 originally? There's almost 5,000 people on it now." That level of interest should keep Mike Orr in music festivals for many summers to come. ■

**Shitar, headstock.** Orr selected maple for the neck and walnut for the headstock 'wings' and fingerboard, and used a Salvation Army necktie as a strap.

**Shitar, body detail.** The tone and volume knobs, as well as the tail piece, are clearly seen here.

**Shitar.** Mike Orr repurposed an old, enameled bedpan to create this unusual fretless four-string electric guitar.

# LENNY PIROTH-ROBERT
## DADDY MOJO GUITARS
### MONTREAL, CANADA

*What started for Lenny Piroth-Robert as a diversion grew into a hobby that then leapt into a craft-based-business, which has attracted the attention of some well-known musicians. I called Lenny at his loft in Montreal.*

"It's been really humbling to see some of the people who have been calling and asking us for instruments."

Lenny Piroth-Robert grew up in Montreal in an artistic, music-friendly environment. His parents ran a firm that designed and constructed show window displays for high-end retailers. Lenny recalls that his first job was building wooden boxes for those window displays. He would also learn the art of decorative painting working in his parents' firm.

Lenny studied fine arts at Dawson College and, upon graduation, worked as an artist from his Montreal studio, selling his paintings through several gallery outlets. "Painting was my real vocation through my twenties. It's a tough way to make a living," he admitted.

Painting was not Piroth-Robert's only love. "I've always been a lover of old blues; I've always kept a guitar around the studio, always played guitar and done a little recording on the side." In autumn 2006, while taking an Internet break from his work, Lenny came across a picture of a guitar someone had built from a cigar box. He felt strongly drawn to that object—in part artistically, but more powerfully by the idea "that someone would want to play music so badly that they would piece something together, just because they had that need to make music. That touched me."

He hit a local tobacconist's shop, scored a pair of cigar boxes, and built a cigar box guitar. "The first one you make, you don't know. Is this going to work? Is it going to sound good? You have absolutely no idea. The response of the instrument acoustically blew me away. It was like instant gratification the second I played it. I'd tuned it in open G or something—three strings—there was sound with the slide and I was like 'Oh My God this works.'"

Encouraged, Lenny built a few more. "At that point, I had absolutely no knowledge of woodworking; I had no tools; I had nothing. I was basically hand carving them with sandpaper, rounding the necks that way. The first one I made had a piezo [pickup], but the frets were drawn on with marker."

**Lenny Piroth-Robert.**
Piroth-Robert demonstrates
a Daddy Mojo eight-string
resophonic prototype.

Initially he just wanted to get it right and build a playable instrument. "I really wasn't worrying about painting or decorative elements at that point." As Lenny gained confidence in the construction and mechanics, he turned his attention to visual aesthetics. He also wanted to share his enjoyment, so he built cigar box guitars for friends and for some musicians he knew.

"It was such a progressive thing. The first couple of months I was making maybe one a month. Then I started listing them on eBay. Back then there was nobody [else selling], maybe one guy—Chicken Bone John in England. I actually wanted to buy one from him, but he wouldn't ship to Canada." For his earliest eBay offerings, Piroth-Robert had the foresight—or audacity— to give his one-man operation a name, and in so doing he created a brand: Daddy Mojo Guitars. "I wanted to grab people's attention with a very descriptive and evocative name that reflected the overall vibe of my instrument." As soon as Piroth-Robert put that first Daddy Mojo cigar box guitar on eBay, it sold. "That was incentive for me. 'Wow, people are digging those,' so I just started making more. I'd make one and put it on eBay. I'd sell it, I'd make another. It kind of started there."

**Tenor resophonic.**
Four-string acoustic tenor guitar with aluminum resonator cone.

By 2007, the demand for his guitars had grown appreciably. Piroth-Robert recruited his friend, artist Luca Tripaldi, for some part-time help. Luca helped develop the Daddy Mojo logo and did prep work on the guitars. He soon took charge of painting and silk-screening, too, and before long he was working full-time for Daddy Mojo. "We developed a lot of designs together. We developed the entire six-string model together," Piroth-Robert related.

Daddy Mojo guitars began upgrading their components and materials, too. In the beginning, Lenny had used poplar for necks, but poplar soon gave way to oak, which he stained dark to give it an aged look. From oak, he soon moved to maple for its more desirable tonal quality. Soon after that, he began adding rosewood fretboards. Though in the beginning he used salvaged tuning machines, Lenny soon moved to buying them new, then to buying better quality machines. Initially, he employed bolts as string nuts, but soon he was buying pre-made plastic nuts. Eventually he moved to carving them himself out of bone. He went from building fretless guitars to building guitars with frets. Initially, he cut the slots for the frets by hand, but before long he had invested some of his cigar box guitar earnings into a table saw, fret guides, and templates. The headstocks evolved, too. He moved from what he calls the "hockey stick" shape to a more traditional guitar shape and began shaping the headstock and tailstock with a router. He also had the Daddy Mojo logo made into decals, just like the major guitar manufacturers.

"At some point we started advertising in different magazines on and off—*Guitar World* and *Vintage Guitar*. Then, a couple of small music stores were interested in carrying some of our instruments. One music store turned into two; into three; into four."

As demand for his guitars drove production up, Lenny had to do some soul searching. "It's something I didn't want to do from the get-go, to standardize. I thought the whole charm of the

## "THE FIRST ONE YOU MAKE, YOU DON'T KNOW. IS THIS GOING TO WORK? IS IT GOING TO SOUND GOOD? YOU HAVE ABSOLUTELY NO IDEA."

instrument was that each box was unique, each instrument personalized, and they were actual boxes that had been used to store cigars; they had that smell and everything.

"At a certain point we had fifteen to twenty stores carrying the line, so we had to standardize the size of the boxes. When you're dealing with building on a case-by-case basis, every cigar box has a different dimension, so the neck has to be fit to that particular box. It's very time consuming, if, let's say, you're doing ten instruments at a time."

"In 2008, I contacted a cigar box manufacturer in the Dominican Republic that actually makes maybe sixty to seventy percent of all the boxes. I sent them some pictures of the instruments we had made and told them, 'you know, we make instruments out of the boxes you manufacture, and we'd love to have you make us a couple of sized boxes for our guitars.' That was

## "A LOT OF PERFORMERS ARE LOOKING TO HAVE AN INSTRUMENT THAT WILL MAKE THEM NOTICEABLE ON STAGE."

another huge upgrade, being able to choose what type of wood was going to go into our boxes, being able to specify the dimensions for sound boxes—the top and bottom are ply cedar and the sides are solid cedar."

Piroth-Robert had his custom cigar boxes branded on the sides with the Daddy Mojo name, much as cigar manufacturers do. He applied his artist's touch and decorative painting skills to give each instrument an aged look. He even had some of his favorite vintage cigar box labels made into decals and silk screens to help define his various lines and make his instruments even more eye-catching and distinctive.

## PIROTH-ROBERT'S INNOVATIVE DRIVE HAS EVEN LED TO SOME, WELL, OUTSIDE-OF-THE-CIGAR-BOX THINKING.

"There were mainly two of us doing this full time for about three years. Then we had a young guy who was studying guitar-making in school who started working here two days a week. He was doing a lot of electronic stuff and some assembly work. At some points there have been four and five people working here full and part time."

Daddy Mojo's expanding crew produced a variety of models with customizable components. "The standard model is a four string. We do four, five, and six. We make three strings only upon request."

Fans of Daddy Mojo guitars, Piroth-Robert explained, fall largely into two camps. "You have some people who like the idea of the cigar box guitar, but they're a little intimidated by the fact that there are only four strings; they don't really know how to approach that. They usually go for the six-string models. The six-string models also cater to a lot of guys that do stage work. They're used to working with a six-string instrument, [and] they don't feel like dealing with the learning curve of a four-string instrument."

"There's the other spectrum: people who have more of a purist attitude, and the whole point to them of a cigar box guitar is that it's bare bones; a limited number of strings. A lot of those guys don't even want a magnetic pickup— they want a piezo or no pickup at all. It's split in terms of popularity between the four-string and six-string."

Daddy Mojo's highly evolved cigar box guitars don't seem that far removed from commercially available electric guitars. Asked what the cigar box actually contributes when it's the basis for a six-string electric with magnetic pickups and an adjustable steel truss-rod in the neck, Piroth-Robert wavers. "The cigar

**Daddy Mojo resophonic.**
This is the prototype of the DM four-string tenor resophonic.

box actually acts as a hollow body…I think it's more of a sense of history than a realistic sound contribution at that point. I really think it's a love for that romantic notion or concept of cigar box guitars and it being translated to an instrument that you can play like a standard guitar. It's sort of a mix. I know a lot of purists think the six-string model is a bit of an overkill."

Lenny adds that the look of the instrument can also attract buyers. "A lot of performers are looking to have an instrument that will make them noticeable on stage. I hear that a lot: 'There are so many acts in my city; it's important to have instruments that'll attract attention.'"

Asked if guitar building leaves him any time to play, Piroth-Robert responded enthusiastically. "Yeah, absolutely. I play every day. I'm the one who tunes all the guitars and does all the setups. I've actually become a much better player than I ever was because I play so much!"

After several years of building 300 guitars a year, more soul searching was in order. Piroth-Robert began to feel his guitars were being mass-produced. "They weren't—there were only two guys in the studio, but . . ." he reflected, and then, in thoughtful understatement, explained, "I reached a point where I knew how to make a four-string cigar box guitar.

"For me, it was also a creative thing. When you've made 700 or more [four-string] cigar box guitars, there's not really any point continuing. I'd rather do something else; it's sort of a natural evolution." That creative drive gave birth to a five-string model, which Lenny said about ten percent of his clients go for.

"A lot of guys who are into open G on the slide will go for the five-string. In open G, a lot of times you won't really use the bass string. Keith Richards, when he uses the open G tuning, he just completely removes the E string and uses the five remaining strings. Before we had the six-string model, the five-string was actually really popular because it was the closest thing clients could get to a six string. When we came out with

the six-string model, people either opted for the six string or stayed with the four string."

"We're meeting a lot of musicians through the cigar box guitars we're working on…they come to the shop and often we're asked to develop an instrument for a certain application or a certain show or for recording. That's really exciting, too. I'd love to do more hands-on collaboration with musicians in terms of developing instruments for them."

Not everyone who buys a Daddy Mojo guitar intends to play it. "I come from an art background, so a portion of our clientele are collectors and view [our guitars] as art objects. Even in terms of the design on the instrument,

**Tenor resophonic, headstock.** Detail of Martin-style slotted headstock.

the color, the paint, aging—I like things when they look old. It's an art, in terms of aging metal or aging wood, making it look like it's actually lived a lifetime. So that's a lot of fun, too. With my background in painting, it's fun to incorporate different techniques into instrument building."

---

## "MY LIFE HAS CHANGED COMPLETELY SINCE I DISCOVERED CIGAR BOX GUITARS, BOTH ARTISTICALLY AND IN TERMS OF THE WORK I DO. IT'S BEEN A GIFT."

---

Pricing, he admits, is quite subjective. "I know cigar box guitar builders who will not sell anything for under $700, and then there's the opposite—those who won't sell anything for over $200. For me it was a choice that had to be made . . . how can I offer a range of instruments that can be affordable but can also go in a higher range? I always wanted to have both ends to offer." He's managed thus far to keep his basic model within reach for most guitar enthusiasts. "For $295, you can get something that's hand-crafted and uses a good selection of woods and materials.

"Right now I'm trying to bring the company in a new direction. The number of instruments we're making is getting smaller and smaller every year because our instruments are getting more and more intricate. Some of them are a little bit more expensive, so you're selling fewer guitars but spending more time working on them. It's more gratifying as a builder.

"I'm really excited about the Resophonic models. They're still at a prototype stage," Lenny explained. Daddy Mojo's Resophonic prototypes incorporate an aluminum resonator cone, like a Dobro, for a distinctive sound and increased volume without electronic amplification. "We've only done two—one six string and one four string—so there's still fine-tuning to do. I'm also hand carving the necks now—before, all the necks were being cut with routers, so I'm trying to combine traditional luthiers' ways of working, and trying to bridge the gap between cigar box guitar building and traditional guitar building."

Inspired by a photo of an old nine-string, parlor-style guitar, Piroth-Robert recently began a prototype for a nine-string Resophonic. He explained, "It's like a 12-string guitar, but the three bass strings aren't doubled. With nine tuners to line up, it makes for a really interesting, asymmetrical headstock. I don't know how many we'll sell. Talk about a niche market—a nine-string resonator cigar box guitar—but I'm really excited about making the prototypes."

Piroth-Robert's innovative drive has even led to some, well, outside-of-the-cigar-box thinking. With the skills he's acquired building ever more sophisticated guitars, Lenny has naturally thought about crossing over into the land of the mainstream guitar. "I'd really like to start a line of electric guitars . . . solid body and semi-hollow body. Right now I'm working on maybe five different electric guitar prototypes that have nothing to do with cigar box guitar building. I'm reading a lot of books and trying out different shapes. I'm a huge fan of early parlor guitars, so I'm trying to incorporate those shapes into electric guitar making."

That chance encounter with an image that pleased his eye and tugged at his heart has set Lenny Piroth-Robert down a path he could not have imagined when he was a boy building, of all things, wooden boxes for his parents' window displays. "My life has changed completely since I discovered cigar box guitars, both artistically and in terms of the work I do. It's been a gift." ∎

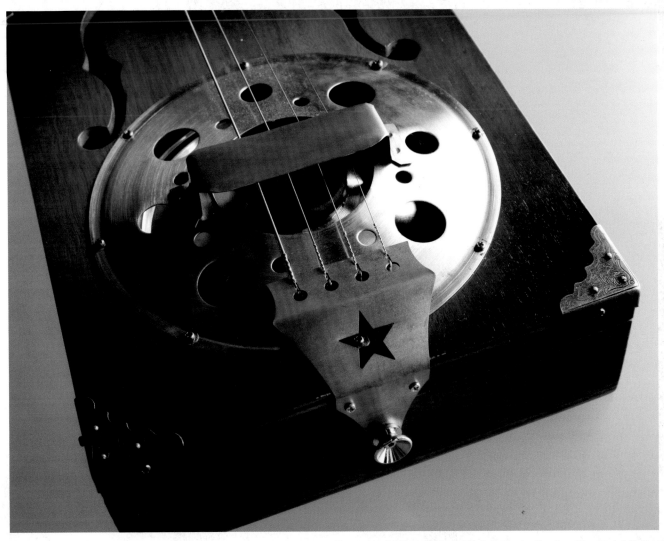

**Tenor resophonic, tail piece.** Detail of resonator, biscuit, and handmade tail piece.

"[I found] a video of a musician wailing away on a three-string guitar. The sound was primitive, gritty, and mean. At the same time, it was almost a spiritual experience. It made the hair stand up on the back of my neck. I was rediscovering music and the real roots of blues for the first time. The cigar box guitar has changed the way I look at music forever."

**—WADE, HANDMADE MUSIC CLUBHOUSE**

# DAVID WILLIAMS
## TELFORD, PENNSYLVANIA

*I met with David Williams in Huntsville, Alabama, the morning of the Sixth Annual Cigar Box Guitar Extravaganza in 2010. David hasn't built many cigar box guitars—the first one he built came out well and he plays it masterfully—but he's built a lot of diddley bows and enjoys teaching others how to build them.*

*In general, David focuses more on playing the instruments he's built. In Huntsville, Alabama, and again in York, Pennsylvania, I had the pleasure of watching David perform both on his cigar box guitar and, as "One String Willie", on his diddley bow.*

Whether it's in a music store or at one of his performances, David Williams gets a kick out of watching people's reactions to his cigar box guitar and his diddley bow. "I've been at places where I've played my cigar box guitar and someone will say, 'Damn! I've got a Strat, and I've spent thousands of dollars trying to get the sound that you have.' I didn't have the heart to tell him that it's all in your hands."

"You go into a guitar store, you lust after multi-thousand-dollar instruments, your Martins, your Taylors, Collings, or Fender Les Pauls; maybe a Paul Reid Smith or a Parker Fly. I had a Parker Fly on my radar screen as a guitar I would love to have—but I'd never own it. At that point it would not be possible for me to become a better guitarist; it was just a cool guitar.

"The cool thing about the cigar box guitar has nothing to do with creativity but does have to do with your attitude. Many intermediate-level guitarists think, 'If only I had a better guitar, I would be a better player,' just like many intermediate-level golfers think, 'If only I had better clubs, I'd be a better golfer.' After building and playing the cigar box guitar, you . . . [realize that] actually what you need to do is to work on just learning to play the guitar that you have."

**David Williams.**
David Williams, aka
One String Willie.

David Williams was born in Champaign, Illinois, in 1949, and came of age during the Folk Revival. He wanted to join in and learn to play guitar, so for his fifteenth birthday, his parents rented a guitar and gave him a six-pack of lessons. Six weeks later, David turned in his rental and bought his first guitar for $15.

The following summer, his family moved to the Washington, D.C., area, where he and his brother, a banjo player, continued to cultivate their interest in music and to develop their playing skills.

"My brother would be buying string band albums by the New Lost City Ramblers and I would be buying country blues and electric blues albums. We put together a string band with my father playing a homemade washtub bass." That line-up still performs bluegrass tunes at Williams' parents' church.

Williams was brought up with a strong sense of duty to country, so when he moved on to the University of Maryland after graduating from high school in 1967, he signed up for ROTC. With the draft in full swing, enlisting in ROTC

**One String Willie.**
David Williams performing as his alter-ego, One String Willie, at the 2010 Cigar Box Guitar Extravaganza in Huntsville, Alabama.

also served as a hedge in case he washed out academically. Far from washing out, Williams earned a BS in chemistry from the University of Maryland in 1971. One hour after graduating, he says, he was a second lieutenant in the U. S. Air Force.

While serving as a munitions officer in the Air Force, Williams kept his Gibson D45-12 twelve-string acoustic guitar close by, playing in his spare time in southern California and the Philippines.

## "EVERYBODY'S REALLY SURPRISED AT HOW GOOD [MY CIGAR BOX GUITAR] SOUNDS."

"When I was in the military, I was kind of flush with money, and so just before I went to the Philippines I bought a nice Martin guitar and I hid it under my bed at my parents' house. I was sort of embarrassed that I had that good of a guitar because I was not that good of a player. I sort of

hoped that my skills would grow into the guitar, which I think they sort of did. I now consider myself a relatively good intermediate player."

After he'd done his part for his country, Williams went to the University of Iowa. While working on his PhD, he took an interest in slide guitar playing and applied himself to learning that. He completed a PhD in biochemistry in 1981, then moved on to the National Institutes of Health, where he completed a post-doctorate in 1985. Once his post-doc was completed, he settled into working for "big pharma" for the next 24 years, retiring in March 2010, just a few months before we met.

"I had been interested in guitar building and I'd ended up with about a foot and a half of bookshelf space filled with books about guitar building and lutherie. I never pulled the trigger on it because just to buy the raw materials for a guitar ends up in the $100-$150 range, and there's no guarantee what it's going to sound like."

In 2004, one of the guys David worked with showed him an article in the local paper about

Shane Speal and cigar box guitars. "I thought, 'How hard could this be?'"

All he lacked to build a cigar box guitar was tuners. "I ordered tuners from Elderly Instruments. The tuners arrived on a Wednesday and I built the guitar Thursday and Friday nights." Indicating his well-played cigar box guitar, he says, "This is my 'Number One.'" He thought he might as well make it look nice, so he fancied up the shape of his sound holes and headstock just a bit. "That was pretty much all done with non-powered tools, except for cutting out the little decoration on the headstock, which I did with a band saw and an electric drill. Most of the rest was done with hand tools. The strap: I think it's a Coach belt that I got at the thrift store for a dollar. Someone was a really heavy guy, and I ended up with a nice strap. The total cost was less than the list price of most CDs. And it's electric."

It looked nice, sure, but how good could it sound? David wondered. So he strung it up and tuned it. "It actually sounds pretty good. Everybody's really surprised at how good it sounds. I have four strings on it, which I have tuned to the top four strings on a six-string guitar, D–G–B–E*. It doesn't have any frets, so I play it slide style. There are two basic slide tunings. There's open G (or A), which is called Spanish, and the other one is Open E (or F), which is called Sevastopol. I tried the Spanish tuning and the Sevastopol tuning, and I really did not like the Sevastopol tuning. The Spanish tuning was much better for this small number of strings. The Sevastopol, I tend to use the bass strings much more, but the Spanish works for me up in the treble strings.

"So you've got an instrument that looks like shit, OK? It doesn't sound like a Martin or a Taylor or a Strat or a Les Paul. I decided what I needed to do to make this work was to become a master of playing that instrument. The way I was looking at it, you want the audience expectation to be really low. Then you want to blow their socks off with the playing."

Williams is nothing if not methodical. "I decided the only way I'm going to master this is to ignore all my other instruments." Packing away his six- and twelve-string guitars for most of four years, Williams devoted himself almost exclusively to mastering the cigar box guitar.

## "YOU CAN MAKE A GUITAR OR OTHER MUSICAL INSTRUMENT, AND YOU CAN MAKE REALLY GOOD MUSIC COME OUT OF IT FOR NEXT TO NO MONEY AT ALL."

That approach has paid off. "I think without setting aside the other instruments, I would have held back. After fifteen months or so, I had pretty much achieved the level of skill that I'm probably going to have."

Williams built his "#1" on June 14, 2004. By the following summer, he was ready to rumble. He'd been corresponding with Shane Speal, Gerry Thompson, Johnny Lowebow, and a number of other players, and learned they were putting together a Cigar Box Guitar festival in Red Lion, Pennsylvania. "Red Lion is just two hours away from me. They offered to let me play a few songs between sets, so I did. The following year at Red Lion, I was on the bill."

Williams had barely settled into performing on the cigar box guitar when Shane Speal infected him with another idea. In early spring 2006, Speal told Williams about a CD by someone named Eddie "One String" Jones. "He said, 'You've gotta listen to this CD. He plays a diddley bow.'"

"I knew what a diddley bow was because I had read about them in multiple blues books.

*Williams tunes the D–G–B–E strings of the standard guitar to D–F#–A–D or open D.

I thought I might make one some day, but I wasn't really into it. That was before I got interested in cigar box guitars, and this is why the cigar box guitar is an important transition. I realized you can make a guitar or other musical instrument, and you can make really good music come out of it for next to no money at all. At that point, a diddley bow is much more on the radar screen. A cigar box guitar is relatively simple to make, but it's a heck of a lot more complicated than a diddley bow."

---

## "THE QUESTION IS, HOW DO YOU MASTER AN INSTRUMENT FOR WHICH THERE'S NO INSTRUCTION BOOKS WHATSOEVER?"

---

Shane's inspiration had been an album called *One String Blues* by Eddie "One String" Jones and Edward Hazelton. "They were discovered by some sort of musicologist back in the early sixties, playing on Skid Row." Jones plays the diddley bow and sings while Hazelton plays the harmonica.

"I LOVED the music—The music is really, really raw, but it's really cool, too. I listened to it and I thought, 'OK, let's make one of these.' So I built one. The night before the second Red Lion gig, I showed it to Shane. I had used a paint-can resonator. I showed him that I had started to learn how to play it. Shane says to me, 'You have got to incorporate this into your act.' Donald Bostwick heard about it and the two of them convinced me that I should learn how to do this.

"Shane's very much a cheerleader; he encourages people to find their muse, to have the guts to build your stuff, record your stuff, and that if it sounds good to you, it IS good. That's the kind of atmosphere Shane has encouraged all along. He's really the guy who got me over

the hump and got me going on the diddley bow." This was August 2006.

"Eddie Jones was Eddie 'One String' Jones. My last name is Williams. In the military, if your name is Brown, you're Brownie; if it's Smith, you're Smitty. My nickname had been Willie, so I said if I'm going to do this, then I'm going to be One String Willie.

"Eddie was a street musician. I wanted a name that would of evoke that kind of person. I actually decided I would try to develop a stage persona that would be like a street musician, but would not be in any way offensive to either homeless people or African Americans. That's how this came about."

With his characteristic focus, Wiliams decided he'd either master the diddley bow or not do it at all. Once again he put his main instrument—this time the cigar box guitar—on ice, and devoted himself to learning to play the diddley bow.

"The question is, how do you master an instrument for which there's no instruction books whatsoever? It took a lot of experimentation. The first question is how many different sounds can you get out of one string? How many different ways can you get those sounds? That took some experimentation. I started out trying to work out some riffs based on the Eddie Jones recording and then moved beyond that."

Williams continues to marvel at just how much music he can get out of simple, simple instruments. "The very first time I strung up the cigar box guitar and heard the first few notes coming out of it I thought, 'Damn! This sounds good!' But then, the diddley bow!" David shakes his head in wonder at how little it takes to produce musical sounds. He adds, "It's been a lot of fun."

As One String Willie, Williams coaxes quite a range of sounds from his diddley bow. With the instrument on his lap, he uses a short length of pipe to tap out rhythms with his right hand while changing tones by means of a bottle slide in his left hand. He's found he can increase his range and add rhythms by using both edges of a flat bottle (see image on page 204) and turning his wrist as he plays.

In addition to donning a watch cap and dark glasses and cultivating his diddley bow playing, Williams started writing songs that would go along with his One String Willie persona.

"One of the important things about the cigar box guitar—you've made your own instrument, why should you NOT make your own music? It forces you to do that. The One String Willie persona provides inspiration for some of the songs. You have to imagine One String Willie. I start with a song. I add stuff to the song, then I take away some of the original stuff. I add stuff, take away more original stuff, 'til finally there's nothing left of the original song. The tune might have changed along the way, too, because some tunes are easier to play on the diddley bow than others. I wrote a bunch of songs that way."

In spite of the fact that he'd concentrated most of his forty years of guitar playing on the blues, Williams acknowledges he doesn't really fit the "blues man" profile. "I really like a lot of the guys, but I'm not personally experienced with the kinds of sorrows that they sing about."

This realization has led One String Willie to write the type of "preposterous bragging songs" that Muddy Waters was fond of. "Those I like because they sort of strut, it's not 'poor me', it's tongue in cheek."

One of Williams' more successful diddley bow songs he calls "One String Willie goes to Europe." "The idea is that One String Willie is the kind of guy that you might run into in a bar who tells amusing stories that almost certainly aren't true. The story is the U.S. sends One String Willie as the Cultural Ambassador to Europe. He meets the Pope, gives career advice to him; he

meets the *King* of England—the closest he's ever been to a king, of course, is in a deck of cards. The joke comes in at the very end, when he plays his one-string for the King: 'the King and Queen they asked him back/to play his one-string for the Jack.' Those are the kind of songs. Light-hearted, tongue in cheek."

Williams enjoys the way his musical explorations all intertwine. "It all sort of comes together. I had been pretty active in the music group in our church . . . a lot of gospel stuff started to come up through me. I was trying to make it so we had a much more diverse musical program in this little acoustic group. So going from old blues, I moved into old gospel records; I got interested in shape

**"#1."** Williams still plays the first CBG he built. He added the coat hook to shift the instrument's center of gravity to offset the weight of the neck and balance the guitar.

> "FOR CREATIVITY, [THE CIGAR BOX GUITAR] KIND OF JUMPS YOU OUT OF THAT MUSICAL RUT. YOU'VE GOT TO GO WITH WHAT THE INSTRUMENT CAN DO; YOU'VE GOT TO WORK OUT HOW TO MAKE THE MUSIC THAT'S IN YOUR HEAD COME OUT OF THE INSTRUMENT."

note music, and older African American music. About a year after I started playing the cigar box guitar, we needed something for the church talent show. I started thinking about classic pieces like 'Amazing Grace.'"

Inspiration struck while Williams was doing the chemist's equivalent of watching paint dry: cultivating cell cultures. "This can be very boring. You add some stuff to the flask, then you have to sit there for a certain amount of time for the enzymes in there to loosen up the cells. You can't force it, so you're sitting there waiting, all kinds of noisy fans blowing in the tissue culture hood. I was the only person in this fairly small room, so I would just sing out loud to myself." That setting proved fertile ground for cultivating

not just cells, but songs as well. Williams' cigar box guitar tune "The New Amazing Grace" came right out of his cell culture lab. "I was writing the verses with a lab marker on paper towels. I stuffed that in my lab coat pocket, then typed it up later. Over the course of the next few days I figured out three new verses to 'Amazing Grace' to perform on the cigar box guitar—that's my 'New Amazing Grace.'"

"For creativity, [the cigar box guitar] kind of jumps you out of that musical rut. You've got to go with what the instrument can do; you've got to work out how to make the music that's in your head come out of the instrument. I find it very hard to play 'The New Amazing Grace' on a regular guitar."

All these things coming together, cross-pollinating in this way, also provide David Williams with more opportunities to shock and amaze the general public. "There's no more amusing thing to do than take a cigar box guitar—or better still a diddley bow—into a guitar store and try out effects pedals. I did that recently because I wanted to get a reverb for my diddley bow. The guys did not know what to say at all. They were just flabbergasted." ∎

"I'm a little worn around the edges and so are my instruments. It seems that most folks try to polish and sterilize every bit of their existence these days, but pulling together bits and pieces to build a cigar box guitar, and to wrap our hands around a primitive instrument, puts us back in touch with the dirt, the sun, and the heartbeat of our souls."

—DAWN VENTIMIGLIA, CIGAR BOX NATION

**Sisters, detail.** Closeup showing the bridge and screw-eye used as a string anchor.

**Sisters, headstocks.** Slotted headstocks and mechanical tuning machines.

**Sisters: Twin examples of cigar box diddley bows.** These are two historic examples of diddley bows. Though these two diddley bows came from different sources, Bill Jehle calls them sisters because they were clearly built by the same maker. Discovered at two separate auctions, they date to the 1930s and came from upstate New York. Each has a single mechanical guitar tuner and otherwise all wood construction.

# Rolling Your Own:
# BUILDING A HOMEMADE ELECTROMAGNETIC GUITAR (OR DIDDLEY BOW) PICKUP
## BY ONE STRING WILLIE

## MATERIALS AND TOOLS

- Singer Class 15 plastic sewing machine bobbins (the central hole diameter varies slightly with bobbin type—Class 15 fits the magnets below)
- ¼" (6mm)-diameter, ½" (13mm)-long cylindrical neodymium magnets (I recommend *www.wondermagnet.com*)
- 42 AWG single build copper magnet wire, such as from *www.stewmac.com*. 30 AWG magnet wire, such as that from Radio Shack, should also work.
- Blue painter's masking tape
- 600-grit emery paper
- Scissors
- Sewing machine
- Platform slightly lower than the bobbin winder with a rounded edge, covered with felt
- Piece of wool felt
- Small weight (~4–5 oz.), like a stack of quarters or large washers
- Clean and empty one-quart metal paint can

- 1 lb. paraffin (sold in grocery stores for canning)
- 4 oz. beeswax (sold in craft stores for making candles)
- ½" (6mm) waterproof adhesive tape (sold for bandages)
- Magnetic compass
- Multimeter (volt ohm meter)
- Soldering iron and acid-free solder
- Brass escutcheon pins
- 22 AWG two conductor shielded audio cable, 12" (305mm)-long (such as Radio Shack part #278-513)
- ¼" (6mm) phono jack
- Saw
- Screwdriver
- Scissors
- Ruler
- Razor blade
- Silicone caulk or hot glue
- Pot for hot water

When I first started building homemade instruments, I used a piezoelectric buzzer from Radio Shack (273-073A) as a pickup for electrifying the instrument (see *www.onestringwillie.com* for details). While cheap and simple, a piezo transducer has some downsides: It has a low signal output compared to an electromagnetic pickup; it picks up a lot of handling noise and can go into uncontrollable feedback in high volume situations; and it sounds thin—it

is okay to reinforce an acoustic sound, but is not nearly as authoritative as an electromagnetic pickup for highly amplified applications.

If you want to crank it up to where it sounds like you really DO have possession over Judgment Day, an electromagnetic pickup is the way to go. Here, I describe how to wind your own single-pole electromagnetic guitar pickups on a sewing machine bobbin.

## I. Wind the Bobbin

**1** Find the end of the wire, and use a small piece of blue masking tape to stick it to the end of the spool so you can find it. 42 AWG magnet wire is only about 0.0025" (.0635mm) in diameter—not much different than a human hair. If you lose the end of the wire, it is really difficult to find it again. Therefore, any time you cut the wire, make sure that the end coming from the spool is stuck down with the tape BEFORE you cut. Set the spool aside.

**2** Learn how to use your sewing machine's bobbin winder. Near the bobbin winder post is a small metal finger called a brake that pushes on the bobbin when it gets full of thread (Figure A). You don't want the brake to push on your bobbin of wire, so I suggest you remove this brake before winding your pickups. Typically, the brake is held on with a small screw and nut, and the nut is on the *inside* of the machine. Make sure you can retrieve the nut *before* you try to remove the brake—don't lose the nut into the machinery.

**Figure A.** The bobbin winder and the brake above it that stops the winding when the bobbin gets full. You will need to remove the brake.

**Figure B.** Build a wooden platform with a rounded edge that will sit on the work surface at the height of the top of the sewing machine, a little lower than the bottom of the bobbin winder, and hanging over the edge of the work surface.

**3** Set up the sewing machine fairly far back on your work table. Put the foot pedal on the table in front of the machine.

**4** Build a wooden platform with a rounded edge that will sit on the work surface at the height of the top of the sewing machine, a little lower than the bottom of the bobbin winder, and hanging over the edge of the work surface (Figure B). Cover the rounded edge of the platform with felt. The spool of magnet wire sits underneath this edge on the floor. The wire comes up from the spool, over the felt-covered, rounded edge of the platform, and then onto the bobbin mounted on the bobbin winder post, allowing the wire to feed straight onto the bobbin and providing some room to maneuver the wire to even the feed (A length of yarn is used in Figure C to clearly show the wire path).

**Figure C.** Here, a length of yarn shows how the wire comes up from the spool, over the felt-covered rounded edge of the platform, and then onto the bobbin mounted on the bobbin winder post.

**Figure D.** Tape the end of the wire down on the platform and lightly rub its free end with 600-grit emery paper.

**Figure E.** Thread some wire through the top hole of the bobbin and tape it down.

**Figure F.** Run the wire over the rounded and felt-padded part of the platform, and put a piece of felt with the weights over top of it.

**5** Before threading the wire onto the bobbin, tape the end of the wire down on the platform and lightly rub its free end with 600-grit emery paper for a couple of strokes to remove the insulation, so you can solder it later (Figure D).

**6** Thread about 2" (51mm) of wire through the small hole in the top side of the bobbin, and hold it in place on the top with a very small piece of blue masking tape (Figure E).

**7** Near the felt-covered rounded edge of the platform, place another small piece of felt on top of the wire and then place a small weight on top of the felt: the wire is sandwiched between two pieces of felt, and the weight allows a constant resistance for the bobbin winder to pull against (Figure F). For me, weights between 50g and 200g (2oz to 7oz) worked well. Put a few very small pieces of painter's tape somewhere on the platform so they will be available when you cut the wire.

**Figure G.** Wind the bobbin until it is nearly full.

**Figure H.** Remove the bobbin from the winder and tape down the ends.

**8** Using your left hand to control the foot pedal, carefully wind the wire onto the bobbin, moving it up and down slightly with your right hand to distribute it fairly evenly. There is a narrow rim on the bobbin, and I fill it to this point (Figure G). When the bobbin is filled, tape the long wire onto the platform, and use emery paper to strip the insulation from it, rubbing toward the bobbin. Cut the wire in the middle of the stripped area, holding onto the wound bobbin with your fingers.

**9** Take the bobbin off the winder, holding the wire coil in place, and wind the remainder of the wire onto the bobbin toward the top side of the bobbin (where the original end of the wire is taped down), leaving a tail about 2" (51mm) long. Remove the tape from the original wire coming from the top of the bobbin, and tape the tail onto the edge of the top side, leaving the center hole open (Figure H).

**10** Repeat these instructions to wind as many bobbins as you have patience for—the wire is very fragile, and the pickups are easy to damage until they are mounted, so it is good to have spares (Figure I).

**Figure I.** Wind as many bobbins as you have patience for.

## II. Check the Resistance of the Coils

Use a multimeter to check the resistance between the two ends of the wire on the bobbin. In eight bobbins, I got an average resistance of 1360 ohms, with a variance of 3%. For three of the other bobbins, I allowed the wire to go above the bobbin and it got caught on the tape. Two were useable (but well below the average resistance of the others) and one was not. To ensure domestic tranquility, put the brake back on the sewing machine when you are finished winding.

**1** Outside the house, put 16 oz. solid paraffin and 4 oz. solid beeswax into a clean, empty, one-quart paint can. Inside the house, boil water in a heavy pot on the stove. Take the pot outside, put it on a cork pad, and then place the can of wax in the pot (Figure J). While the wax melts, heat another pot of water, and keep alternating pots of near-boiling water until the wax is completely melted (Figure K). Stir the melting wax with a wooden paint stirrer. The point here is that the can of wax is outside, and the water is heated inside the house. The can of wax is never near the fire.

**2** Thread a loop of heavy wire through the center holes of the wound bobbins (Figure L) and dip them into the wax. Let them sit in the wax until bubbles stop coming out of the windings, indicating the wax has penetrated the windings. Pull the bobbins out of the liquid wax, and let them air-cool over a paper towel.

## III. Pot the Coils in Wax

Pot the coil assemblies in hot wax (by weight, 80% paraffin, 20% beeswax). Potting reduces microphonics—sounds made when the wires in the pickup pick up mechanical vibrations from the guitar/sound system.

**WARNING:** The vapors this wax mixture gives off when it is hot are HIGHLY FLAMMABLE. To minimize the fire hazard, do this step outside. Do not allow anyone to smoke near the hot wax.

**Figure J.** Heat the wax mixture with hot water.

**Figure K.** My outside waxing setup. Make sure you have potholders!

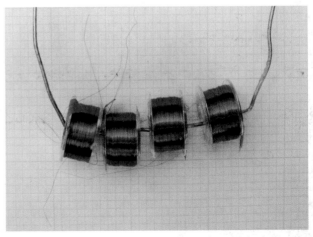

**Figure L.** String the bobbins onto a heavy wire and dunk them in the wax.

**Figure M.** Tape around the wire.

**Figure N.** Use a magnetic compass to mark the polarity of each magnet.

## IV. Add Magnets to Make Pickups

**1** Cut some waterproof adhesive tape (the kind they use for bandages) about 2 ½" (65mm) long and about 9mm (⁵⁄₁₆") wide to fit between the sides of the bobbin. Using a metal ruler and razor blade makes a neat job of it (Figure M).

**2** Wrap the wire coils with the tape to protect them from damage. When applying the tape, try to get both wires on the same face of the bobbin. Write the resistance of the coil on the tape with permanent marker.

**3** Use a magnetic compass to mark the polarity of each magnet, and then insert the magnet into the center hole of the bobbin. Make sure that the magnetic poles for each magnet are all pointing in the same direction with respect to the side of the bobbin where the inside end of the wire comes out. (The exception to this is if you are preparing a pair of coils for a humbucking pickup—see Going Further.)

**Figure O.** Drill two small holes in a piece of very thin plywood. Insert two brass escutcheon pins on the underside of the plywood to use as soldering posts.

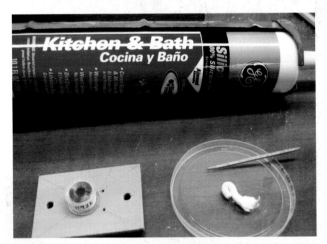

**Figure P.** Use silicon to attach the bobbin to the plywood.

**Figure Q.** Solder the leads to the pins.

## V. Wire the Pickups

**1** To mount the pickups for wiring, drill two small holes in a piece of very thin plywood. Insert two brass escutcheon pins on the underside of the plywood to use as soldering posts (Figure O). Pass the magnet wire leads through the holes, and mount the bobbin using a dab of hot glue or silicone caulk (Figure P).

**2** After carefully sanding the coating off the ends of the wire, solder the leads to the escutcheon pins (Figure Q). Prepare a short length of shielded cable by cutting a couple of inches of insulation off each end of the cable, separating the strands of the shielding (Figure R) and cutting off all but a dozen or so strands of the shielding at each end. The shielding strands were twisted together with the stripped black conductor on each end. (If you use plain wire instead of cable, keep the wire lengths short from the soldering posts to the soldering lugs on the ¼" [6mm] phono jack.)

**3** Solder one end of the cable to the escutcheon pins and the other onto the lugs of the phono jack (Figure S). Solder the black conductor/shielding onto the lug that connects to the barrel of the phono plug, not the tip. Use the digital volt ohm meter to make sure the connections are good.

"The building of Cigar Box Guitars will turn a hardcore germophobe into an all-out dumpster divin' fool in about three days. It's the nature of the beast. Join the cigar box guitar revolution!"

**—SHANE HOPKINS,
HANDMADE MUSIC CLUBHOUSE**

**Figure R.** Prepare a short length of shielded wire.

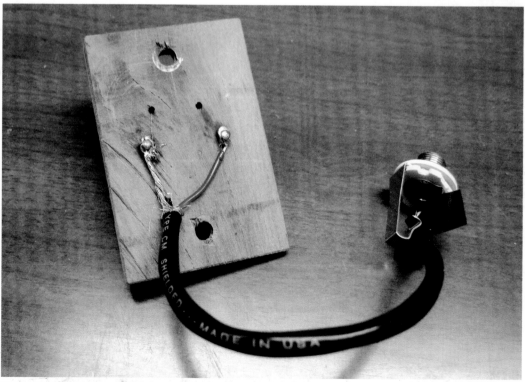

**Figure S.** Solder one end of the cable to the escutcheon pins and the other onto the lugs of the phono jack.

## VI. Mount the Pickups

You can work out for yourself how to attach this assembly to your instrument, but remember that the fine wires from the coil break easily if the coil is jarred loose from the plywood—make sure you mount it so the coil and wires are protected. One pickup will be good for one string (mounted directly beneath the string) or two strings (mounted directly between the strings). For more strings, wire the pickups in series—the outside wire of one pickup connected to the inside wire of the next.

## Going Further

With this basic pickup winding technique in hand, you can experiment with different magnet types, perhaps using a steel screw as the pole piece with the magnet underneath the mounting board, and with different wire gauges or different numbers of windings (to get different resistances). To make a humbucking pickup, mount two coils (with similar resistances) to go under one string, and join the two *inside* ends of the wire of the two coils together, inserting the magnets into the two coils with opposite polarities. The free outside ends of the coil wires will be connected to the two-conductor shielded cable.

I hope you have fun with building your own pickups, and hope this will inspire you to build your own instruments as well!

*— David "One String Willie" Williams*

"I found cigar box guitars on eBay while looking for a lap steel. I said to myself, 'I can build one of these,' and I did. That was about five years ago, and I just finished number 225. Why I do it I can't really say, but it's worse than drugs. Once you build one you'll build another one."

**—OTTIE "SKY DOG" NOBLE, HANDMADE MUSIC CLUBHOUSE**

# GERRY THOMPSON
## MOORESTOWN, NEW JERSEY

*New Jerseyan Gerry Thompson performed at the 2010 York, Pennsylvania Cigar Box Guitar Festival. His friend, Arthur Herman, added some spice to the mix with his lap steel guitar. The previous night, the duo had performed in New Jersey. Thompson appears in Max Shore's documentary,* Songs Inside the Box, *shot on location during the 2007 Cigar Box Guitar Extravaganza in Huntsville, Alabama.*

"Just to be able to make your own instrument, write your own songs, and then go out and perform them … That's the totality of music. If I hadn't started making cigar box guitars, I don't think I'd be playing music."

Though his dad had marched for years in Philadelphia's famous Mummers parades, strumming a tiny banjo-mandolin, Gerry Thompson had never played a musical instrument. By the time he inherited his dad's banjo-lin, the instrument looked like it had seen better days.

Somewhere around the turn of the millennium, Thompson got new neighbors and a new idea. A three-member band called April May and the Junebugs (incidentally playing at the York festival the afternoon of our interview) moved in next door to Thompson. Guitarist Dave "Catfish" Fecca not only played guitar, he did some repair work as well. "I had this old banjo/mandolin and I said, 'if you can fix this I'll learn how to play it.' So I did. What a horrible sounding instrument that is . . . so I started playing the 'banjolin,' and quickly realized you can't really sing well with a banjolin."

Thompson found some inspiration when he went out to see a band called The Horseflies. "Their lead guitarist played this four-string guitar. He's wailing away on it, and I thought, 'What is that?' I waited until after the show to ask him and he told me it was a tenor guitar. They made them back during the Jazz Age. It has four strings. So I bought one on eBay the next day." He started fiddling around with the tenor guitar. The instrument he bought needed some work. Trolling the Internet for parts, Thompson ran across Shane Speal's cigar box guitar Web site. "I'm thinking, these aren't tenor guitars, but some of them have four strings. Maybe I could just make one of these.

**Gerry Thompson.**
Gerry started with a banjo-lin and later upgraded to cigar box guitar.

"So I called him up and said, 'What do I do?' Shane and a couple of other guys guided me: 'Get these parts, get a cigar box, do this…' I started making cigar box guitars." Because of the similarities between four-string cigar box guitars and the tenor guitar, Thompson already had an inroad into how to play. "Actually it's very easy to chord; I have pretty arthritic hands."

Thompson had always enjoyed putting his thoughts to paper, and had collected hundreds of his own poems into books. Within three months of learning to play a couple of chords on the cigar box guitar, Gerry Thompson had written three

> "JUST TO BE ABLE TO MAKE YOUR OWN INSTRUMENT, WRITE YOUR OWN SONGS, AND THEN GO OUT AND PERFORM THEM… THAT'S THE TOTALITY OF MUSIC. IF I HADN'T STARTED MAKING CIGAR BOX GUITARS, I DON'T THINK I'D BE PLAYING MUSIC."

**Gerry Thompson.**
Thompson on stage at the Emporium Book Store in York, PA, summer 2010.

songs. "I just needed an outlet, as opposed to writing poems—the idea of being able to express things—it's a wonderful thing."

Performing seemed like the natural next step, but it wasn't necessarily on Thompson's radar screen. "I was dreadfully sick. I had gotten a liver transplant 19 years ago and it was failing when I started playing." In spite of his ill health, Thompson wanted to be on hand for one of the first cigar box guitar festivals, held in Carrollton, Kentucky, in 2006.

## "PLAYING MUSIC IS PROBABLY MY FAVORITE THING IN LIFE."

"One of the guys who now makes very high-end cigar box guitars, Kurt Schoen, had this festival. I talked one of my friends into going with me. I said, "We're going to Kentucky. We're going to a cigar box guitar festival." Thompson and his friend arrived in a downpour and found the organizers struggling to move the stage. Thompson and his pal jumped right in to help. "Me and a couple of other guys I'd only met on the Internet moved the stage and set things up."

Around midday, when Linda Kay and Pearl Handled Pistol were scheduled to go on, Gerry got an unexpected break. "She was having trouble getting set up and this one guy says to me, 'You've got your guitar, get up there and play something so we don't lose the crowd!'

"I had never played in front of ANYbody before. So I got up and played four songs. People were cheering. I thought, 'Wow.' I adapted to being on the stage very easily. I guess I'm naturally full of it. I like to perform. It's fun; I don't take it real seriously. At the end of the day, this guy said, 'I'm having a festival in West Virginia in a couple of months. Why don't you bring your band?' I'm thinking, 'Bring my band?' So I brought my next-door neighbors, who actually play in a blues band. I taught them a whole set of my songs and they backed me up."

In 2007, Gerry got a new lease on life when he received a second liver transplant. Two weeks after the surgery, he hit the road again, making his way to Huntsville, Alabama, for the third annual Cigar Box Guitar Extravaganza. "It didn't slow me down in the least. It gave me something to look forward, to, to concentrate on. It added some purpose where it was needed."

Thompson seems slightly awed by his own success, by just how easily he went from not playing anything to having a hundred of his own songs. "A couple of months ago I opened up for Peter Tork of the Monkees. If [a year ago] someone would have said 'Next year, you're going to open up for Peter Tork of the Monkees,' I would have laughed. How would *I* do that?

"I'm not the best guitar player in the world. I have a very strange voice; it's kind of high and 'interesting.' Before I started playing, I'd be singing along with the radio and people would say, 'Oh God, please don't sing.' But I write catchy little songs and people like them. I can't sing other people's songs, but when I write my own, I can sing to mine. I think everyone has that in them and it's so liberating. It feels so good to be able to do that. I think everybody should experience that. Playing music is probably my favorite thing in life. It's the only time I'm completely relaxed—when I'm sitting at home writing or playing something, or when I'm up on stage, that's the best I feel, when I'm doing that. It's a great outlet. It takes everything away." ∎

# INDEX

ACQUISITION EDITOR:
**PEG COUCH**

COPY EDITOR:
**PAUL HAMBKE**

COVER AND LAYOUT DESIGNER:
**JASON DELLER**

DEVELOPMENTAL EDITOR:
**KERRI LANDIS**

PHOTOGRAPHY, UNLESS OTHERWISE NOTED:
**DAVID SUTTON**

PROOFREADER:
**DEBBIE HENRY**

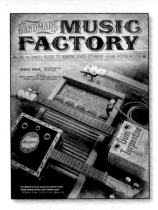
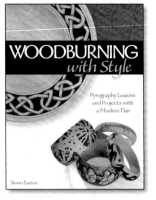

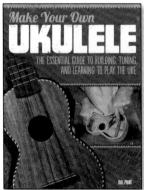